RECOVERING NATURAL LAW

RECOVERING NATURAL LAW

A Guide for Protestants

Benjamin B. Saunders

BakerBooks
a division of Baker Publishing Group
Grand Rapids, Michigan

Published by Baker Books
a division of Baker Publishing Group
Grand Rapids, Michigan
BakerBooks.com

Printed in the United States of America

Library of Congress Cataloging-in-Publication Data
Names: Saunders, Benjamin B., author
Title: Recovering natural law : a guide for Protestants / Benjamin B. Saunders.
Description: Grand Rapids, Michigan : Baker Books, a division of Baker Publishing Group, [2026] | Includes bibliographical references.
Identifiers: LCCN 2026007960 | ISBN 9781540906038 paperback | ISBN 9781493465446 ebook
Subjects: LCSH: Natural law—Religious aspects—Protestant churches | Natural law—Biblical teaching | Christian ethics—Protestant authors | Protestant churches—Doctrines
Classification: LCC BR115.L28 S28 2026
LC record available at https://lccn.loc.gov/2026007960

Cover design by Dustin Kilgore

Baker Publishing Group publications use paper produced from sustainable forestry practices and postconsumer waste whenever possible.

26 27 28 29 30 31 32 7 6 5 4 3 2 1

O LORD, how manifold are your works!
In wisdom have you made them all;
the earth is full of your creatures. . . .
May the glory of the LORD endure forever;
may the LORD rejoice in his works.

Psalm 104:24, 31

The first law of nature itself acknowledges that there is one God, who is eternal mind, wise, just, good, the Creator of things, kind toward the righteous and punitive toward the unrighteous, by whom there has been ingrafted into us the understanding of the difference between good and evil, and that our obedience is based on this distinction; that this God is to be invoked and that good things are to be expected from Him.

Philip Melanchthon

Contents

Contents

Introduction

Many today profess to believe that morality is relative or subjective—that there is no such thing as universal morality or a universal human nature, the body has no intrinsic significance or meaning, our internal feelings are who we really are, and humans are free to shape and reshape their bodies to reflect their true selves. Many believe that law is simply whatever is passed by the lawmaker, subject to no higher standard, and that technology should continue to push the boundaries of the human, with the only constraint being what is possible.

In short, there is widespread disagreement about morality and a lack of confidence in the existence of universal moral truths. What is needed to counter these developments is the recovery of a belief in an overriding, universally applicable standard of morality. This standard would recognize that human nature and the human body have meaning that is objective and given, not infinitely malleable. It would also counter the impulse of technological development and provide a standard by which to hold civil rulers to account. What is needed is a doctrine of natural law.

Natural law was once an important part of Protestant thinking about morality, law, and government but has fallen into neglect. In recent decades there have been increasing calls for Protestants to recover the doctrine of natural law.[1] And yet many Protestants remain skeptical. For Christians, it is thought, Scripture is the only safe guide. Natural law can seem woolly and anthropocentric. For example, Thomas Aquinas, who penned the classic explanation of natural law, wrote that "man has a natural inclination to know the truth concerning God and to live in society; and, accordingly, whatever pertains to this inclination belongs to the natural law: for instance, to shun ignorance, to avoid giving offence to those among whom one has to live, and other such things."[2] In contrast to this, the Ten Commandments are clear, precise, theocentric, authoritative, and convicting. Why do we need Aquinas when we have the clarity of Scripture?

Indeed, if Scripture is the supreme authority, sufficient for faith and life (2 Tim. 3:16–17), why do we need another source of moral teaching? Is natural law merely a lowest common denominator standard of morality? Can we reconcile the doctrine of natural law with biblical teaching? What is the content of natural law? Who has authority to decide that content? How do we know the natural law? Does it propose extrabiblical moral truths that are binding on the conscience? Does natural law posit autonomous human reason? If human reason is corrupted by sin, how can we accurately perceive the natural law? Is natural law a Roman Catholic doctrine? Do we need to accept Aristotelian or Thomist metaphysics in order to hold to natural law?

1. E.g., Carl Trueman, *The Rise and Triumph of the Modern Self: Cultural Amnesia, Expressive Individualism, and the Road to Sexual Revolution* (Crossway, 2020), 405; J. Daryl Charles, "Protestant Bias Against the Natural Law: A Critique," *Journal of Lutheran Ethics* 10, no. 3 (2010).

2. Thomas Aquinas, *Summa Theologica* I-II, 94.2, in *Political Writings*, ed. R. W. Dyson (Cambridge University Press, 2020), 117–18. Hereafter, references to the *Summa Theologica* are cited as *ST*.

This book aims to answer such questions and demonstrate that Protestants need a doctrine of natural law. And yet it is unfamiliar terrain; natural law is a difficult subject, and the history of natural law thinking is complex. Much of the writing about it is the province of specialist scholars focusing on narrow technical questions. Natural law intersects with many different disciplines, including philosophy, theology, biblical studies, ethics, history, jurisprudence, and law, and no mere human can master all these disciplines (my field is that of a law professor).[3]

One conviction of this book is that there is a core set of principles relating to natural law that all Christians ought to be able to accept. Much of the literature on natural law focuses on contested questions around the periphery—such as the technical issues briefly introduced in chapter 7. The complexity of these issues can give the impression that natural law is dauntingly complex and contested. However, notwithstanding disagreement on peripheral questions, there is substantial agreement on the core principles of natural law, and one key aim of this book is to explain those principles.

In this book, my goal is to introduce the subject of natural law from a Protestant perspective. It is aimed principally at Protestant Christians who are unfamiliar with the concept of natural law and is designed to help them understand the concept and its relevance today. I hope to explain how natural law is consistent with Protestant principles and how it can benefit Christians today.

Another purpose of this book is to bring natural law theory and the Bible into conversation. The literature on natural law rarely seems to overlap with biblical scholarship. Much natural law theory seems to pay little attention to the Bible, while

3. Note Immanuel Kant's comments in *Groundwork of the Metaphysics of Morals*, in *Practical Philosophy*, ed. Mary J. Gregor (Cambridge University Press, 1996), 44 [4:388].

biblical studies similarly pays little attention to the natural law tradition. This book aims to present a biblically grounded account of natural law that also has regard to the writings of key natural law theorists.

In developing my account, I draw heavily on the history of Christian thinking about natural law and frequently cite Aquinas and Roman Catholic sources, as well as Protestant writers. In case this poses a stumbling block to readers, I offer the following comments.

I am confessionally Protestant and hold to orthodox Reformed teaching. I cite Roman Catholic sources because there is a much deeper tradition of reflection on natural law within Roman Catholicism than there is in Protestantism, and those sources have much of value to say about natural law. Natural law is a doctrine about which there has been widespread agreement within the Christian tradition, and so historically there has been much common ground among Protestants and Roman Catholics. There is much that Protestants can learn from Roman Catholic writers about natural law. However, nothing in this book should be taken as an endorsement of Roman Catholic teaching about Scripture, tradition, salvation, the sacraments, or the church.

Although I do not consider tradition to be authoritative like Scripture, tradition should nevertheless be taken seriously. This is not to add to Scripture but rather to respect the ongoing work of the Holy Spirit in guiding the church throughout history (John 14:26; 16:13). Theology is the product of the universal church's reflections on Christian doctrine, which occurs within a tradition of historical development.[4] The teaching of

4. Joshua R. Farris, *An Introduction to Theological Anthropology: Humans, Both Creaturely and Divine* (Baker Academic, 2020), 5.

the Christian tradition can be seen as a ministerial authority, subject to the authority of Scripture.[5]

Although only Scripture is truly authoritative, if the overwhelming majority of the Christian church has held something to be true, we ought to be cautious about departing from that teaching, especially if it is enshrined in the creeds and confessions of the church. As Martin Bucer wrote, "Nothing should be hastily repudiated that is commended to us by holy antiquity or by the public consensus of the faithful during so many centuries."[6]

What, then, is natural law?

5. Matthew Barrett, *God's Word Alone: The Authority of Scripture: What the Reformers Taught* (Zondervan, 2016), 346.

6. Martin Bucer, *Common Places of Martin Bucer*, trans. and ed. D. F. Wright (Sutton Courtenay Press, 1972), 40.

1

What Natural Law Is

This chapter provides an overview of the doctrine of natural law. In short, the doctrine of natural law is that there is a universally applicable moral law given by God, and the knowledge of this moral law has been written on every human heart. Conscience and reason are witnesses to this natural law, leading people to act in accord with its precepts. The natural law is the same in fundamental moral content as the Decalogue. It enables people to distinguish between good and evil, notwithstanding that the human ability to discern the natural moral order has been obscured by sin. The laws of human polities ought to be ordered in accordance with the natural law. Natural law is not sufficient for justification or redemption.[1]

Natural Law as Moral Law

Let us start by laying out what should be an uncontroversial definition of *natural law*. Scripture teaches that "all have sinned and

1. This paragraph is drawn from Stephen J. Grabill, *Rediscovering the Natural Law in Reformed Theological Ethics* (Eerdmans, 2006), p. 2 and ch. 1.

fall short of the glory of God" and that all people are condemned by the law (Rom. 3:19–21, 23). Sin is a transgression of God's commands (Lev. 5:17; 1 John 3:4), being "a defect or an inclination or an action in conflict with the law of God."[2] If all people have committed sin, which is a breach of God's commands, this means that all people are subject to a moral law given by God.

The supreme and perfect revelation of the moral law is in Scripture, especially the Ten Commandments (Exod. 20:1–17; Deut. 5:6–21). But many people have not read the Bible and have not read the authoritative revelation of the moral law in the Decalogue. Nevertheless, Scripture tells us that all people have an understanding of that moral law and are accountable for breaching it. Romans 2:14–15, one of the classic texts on natural law, states, "For when Gentiles, who do not have the law, by nature do what the law requires, they are a law to themselves, even though they do not have the law. They show that the work of the law is written on their hearts, while their conscience also bears witness, and their conflicting thoughts accuse or even excuse them."

Earlier, in Romans 1, Paul writes that "the wrath of God is revealed from heaven against all ungodliness and unrighteousness of men, who by their unrighteousness suppress the truth. For what can be known about God is plain to them, because God has shown it to them" (vv. 18–19). That is, all people have knowledge of God but suppress that knowledge in unrighteousness.

These verses teach that there is a moral law that applies to all people at all times. All people have a knowledge of this law because the work of the law is written on the heart (2:14–15). Italian Reformed theologian Girolamo Zanchi writes that "natural law applies to all people. In fact, it is inscribed on every

2. Philip Melanchthon, *The Chief Theological Topics: Loci Praecipui Theologici 1559*, 2nd ed., trans. J. A. O. Preus (Concordia Publishing House, 2011 [1559]), 71.

heart by God himself almost from birth."[3] Our knowledge of that law is always incomplete, because we suppress that truth in unrighteousness (1:18–19). As a result, Scripture is necessary as a more complete and authoritative exposition of the moral law, to correct our defective knowledge.

Our knowledge of the moral law and our ability to carry out its precepts are corrupted by sin, and so natural law cannot provide sufficient knowledge of God for us to be saved or to attain eternal life. It is nevertheless true that humans are able, imperfectly, to perceive moral truths outside of Scripture.

What is the content of this moral law? Christians have traditionally affirmed that the natural law is the same in fundamental moral content as the Decalogue but that the Decalogue and the natural law are not precisely the same in every respect. Chapter 3 discusses the content of natural law in more detail.

In short, Scripture teaches that there is a universally applicable moral law, broadly equivalent in content to the Decalogue and knowable in principle outside of Scripture, although that knowledge is distorted by sin. I refer to this as the *narrow* conception of natural law.

Natural Law as Moral Order

However, the term *natural law* is apt to mislead. This is because natural law is not exclusively or even primarily "law" in the sense of a set of commands or rules to be obeyed, such as "do not commit adultery." Instead, natural law actually means something like a *created order* or *moral order* that is inscribed in the creation. This order can be expressed in certain ways in laws or precepts,

3. Girolamo Zanchi, *On the Law in General*, trans. Jeffrey J. Veenstra (CLP Academic, 2013), 7.

but natural law is broader than those rules. Precepts or rules express some aspects of the moral order but do not exhaust it.[4]

Take, for example, the sixth commandment, "you shall not kill." This reflects the reality that humans are made in the image and likeness of God (Gen. 1:27). Humans have an innate disposition to preserve their lives, and indeed this is considered to be one of the first principles of natural law (see chapter 3). The principle of self-preservation can be fleshed out in numerous ways, and the Pentateuch gives examples of how to apply it in particular cases, such as the parapet law in Deuteronomy 22:8: "When you build a new house, you shall make a parapet for your roof, that you may not bring the guilt of blood upon your house, if anyone should fall from it." In this way, the command "you shall not kill" reflects a broader reality about human nature and the dignity of human life.

Natural law, then, expresses the concept that God has inscribed an order in creation. Lutheran theologian Philip Melanchthon referred to the "beautiful order which has been so wisely established among all creatures" and "the instructions which we have received from the Architect of it all."[5] This reflects the scriptural teaching that God made the world and pronounced it "very good" (Gen. 1:31). The world is not neutral or value-free but has been structured and ordered by God.

Natural law theorists often argue that what is good for something is determined by its nature.[6] Francisco Suárez wrote that the natural law "prescribes that which is good, in so far as the latter involves an intrinsic and necessary connexion with

4. David VanDrunen, *Divine Covenants and Moral Order: A Biblical Theology of Natural Law* (Eerdmans, 2014), 367–68.

5. Melanchthon, *Chief Theological Topics*, 11.

6. Owen Anderson, *The Natural Moral Law: The Good After Modernity* (Cambridge University Press, 2012), ch. 1.

rational nature."[7] Of course, this is not to pit nature against God, as if "nature" is an independent and autonomous force. Rather, as the Creator of everything, God has determined the nature of all things and is the author of the law that reflects that nature.

Natural law is grounded in human nature, aiming to bring humans into conformity with their created nature. Law and order complement each other. Lutheran theologian Niels Hemmingsen put this well: Because "it commands and forbids, it is called 'law,' and because it is implanted in nature, it is called 'natural.'"[8]

The *natural* in *natural law* does not mean "the way things are." Rather, natural law is a normative concept: That is, natural law specifies how things ought to be, consistent with their created nature. The moral order is related to the nature of things, but *natural law* does not refer to the way things habitually act.

Natural law, therefore, is a moral order that is hardwired into human nature and the creation, and can be partially expressed in moral laws or rules. This means that natural law is not primarily a theory but the nature of reality—the way God has made things to be. I refer to this as the *broader* conception of natural law. Chapter 4 discusses the moral order in more detail.

Natural Law and Natural Law Theory

At this point it is important to distinguish natural law from natural law theory. David VanDrunen has written that "natural law is the moral truth God has revealed in the created order and

7. Francisco Suárez, "A Treatise on Laws and God the Lawgiver," in *Selections from Three Works*, ed. Thomas Pink, trans. Gwladys L. Williams et al. (Liberty Fund, 2015), 342; see also 232–40, 293.

8. Niels Hemmingsen, *On the Law of Nature: A Demonstrative Method*, trans. and ed. E. J. Hutchinson (CLP Academic, 2018 [1562]), 29.

made accessible to human minds, while natural law theory is what human beings have thought and taught about the natural law."[9] This helpfully recognizes that there is a distinction between the reality of the natural law (the moral law and created order) and human thinking about natural law, a distinction that is often overlooked.[10] *Natural law* is objective and reflects the nature of reality. Natural law *theory* is fallible and may be in error.

There is a rich history within the Christian tradition of reflecting and writing on the natural law. There is much of value within this tradition, but it is not infallible. Accepting the idea of natural law does not mean that we are bound to accept everything that the Christian tradition has taught about natural law. Indeed, we need not even be wedded to the term *natural law*: other terms such as *creation ethics* or *moral order* express similar truths.

For instance, Thomas Aquinas's account of natural law has been highly influential on Christian thinking and has had a deep impact on both the Roman Catholic and Protestant traditions.[11] His theory of natural law is articulated within an elaborate metaphysical framework that draws from Aristotelian thought. Aquinas's formulations are helpful but not infallible, and by accepting a doctrine of natural law, we are not bound to accept every aspect of Aquinas's account or the Aristotelian metaphysics it draws from.

9. David VanDrunen, "Should Protestants Reject Natural Law? Responding to Common Objections," *Public Discourse*, August 2, 2020, https://www.thepublicdiscourse.com/2020/08/67076.

10. John Finnis, *Natural Law and Natural Rights*, 2nd ed. (Oxford University Press, 2011), 25.

11. The "Treatise on Law," questions 90–97 of the *Summa Theologica* I-II, have been described as "the principal canon for Western natural law jurisprudence." Anthony J. Lisska, *Aquinas's Theory of Natural Law: An Analytic Reconstruction* (Clarendon Press, 1996), 9.

How Do We Know the Natural Law?

The Christian tradition has widely held that the natural law has been written on every human heart and that conscience and reason are witnesses to the natural law. That is, all people have an inbuilt witness to the natural law, and even those who have never been instructed by Scripture can distinguish between good and evil. However, our ability to discern the moral law has been obscured by sin, and so Scripture is necessary as a clearer statement of the moral law to correct our defective knowledge.

Some accounts of natural law seem to treat the natural law and humans' natural knowledge of that law as identical. For instance, the Roman Catholic Church defines *natural law* as "nothing other than the light of understanding placed in us by God; through it we know what we must do and what we must avoid. God has given this light or law at the creation."[12] Similarly, Philip Melanchthon wrote that the law of nature is "the knowledge of the divine law which has been grafted into the nature of man,"[13] and Niels Hemmingsen defined the law of nature as "a certain knowledge, imprinted on the minds of men by God, of the principles of knowing and acting, and of the conclusions proved from these principles that are in agreement with the proper end of man."[14]

One reason for defining natural law in this way is that promulgation is essential to the existence of a valid law, and so human awareness of the natural law is essential for it to exist as a law that binds humans.[15] Nevertheless, it seems preferable

12. *Catechism of the Catholic Church* (St. Pauls Publishing, 1994 [1955]), 475.

13. Melanchthon, *Chief Theological Topics*, 90, 116.

14. Hemmingsen, *On the Law of Nature*, 30.

15. Aquinas defined a law as an "ordinance of reason for the common good, made and promulgated by him who has care of the community": *ST* I-II, 90.4. Another reason for defining natural law in this way is that, according to Aquinas, natural law is the participation by humans in the eternal law, which occurs by means of inclinations imprinted upon human nature: *ST* I-II, 91.2; 94.2.

to distinguish the nature of reality from our knowledge of that reality. Our knowledge of the natural law, which is sometimes described in writings about natural law as the "light of nature," is often in error. That is, it is better to separate "natural law" (the objective moral order) from the "light of nature" (our knowledge of the moral order). Chapter 5 discusses the knowledge of the natural law in more detail.

Natural Law and Civil Law

Another key aspect of the doctrine of natural law is that laws enacted by human civil governments ought to be ordered in accordance with the natural law. Natural law establishes the precepts of the moral law that are in principle knowable to all people. Civil rulers, therefore, are able to discern the precepts of the natural law, which should provide the foundational moral principles for human civil laws.

Natural law is an overriding, objective standard against which human laws can be measured. Civil laws that contravene the natural law are defective and in cases of extreme injustice ought not to be considered laws. However, the natural law is relatively indeterminate, leaving considerable freedom to lawmakers when enacting civil laws.[16] The relationship between natural law and civil law is considered further in chapter 6.

Natural Law and Scripture

Protestants consider Scripture to be the authoritative revelation of the will of God, sufficient for faith and life. The doctrine of natural law raises key questions for Protestants as it relates to

16. See Benjamin B. Saunders, *The Crisis of Civil Law: What the Bible Teaches About Law and What It Means Today* (Lexham Press, 2024), ch. 1.

the role of Scripture, especially: Does natural law undermine the sufficiency of Scripture? And why do we need to affirm the idea of natural law when we have the clarity of Scripture?

Three points should be made about the relationship between Scripture and natural law. First, Scripture itself teaches a principle of natural law—namely, that there is a universal moral order that humans can perceive through their reason and conscience. Anyone who takes the authority of Scripture seriously must affirm something like a doctrine of natural law.

Second, our knowledge of the natural law is corrupted and distorted by sin, and so Scripture is necessary to provide a clear and authoritative restatement of the moral law.

Third, Scripture and natural law should not be pitted against each other but should be seen as mutually illuminating. After all, creation is *God's* world. Scripture presents itself as reality: The Bible contains many passages that are observations on reality and calls us to reflect on the natural order of creation. If natural law and Scripture both reflect the nature of reality, then this means that general and special revelation are complementary means of understanding and interpreting that reality and mutually illuminate each other. Commenting on Psalm 119, Jon D. Levenson writes, "The commandments that the psalmist practices, even those which may be Pentateuchal, constitute a kind of revealed natural law. They enable him to bring his own life into harmony with the rhythm of the cosmos and to have access to the creative and life-giving energy that drives the world."[17]

We should reflect on the world in light of the Word, and the Word in light of the world. Natural law is an invitation to read the book of nature in light of Scripture, and vice versa. In short,

17. Jon D. Levenson, "The Sources of Torah: Psalm 119 and the Modes of Revelation in Second Temple Judaism," in *Ancient Israelite Religion*, ed. P. D. Miller Jr. et al. (Fortress Press, 1987), 559, 569.

natural law is an invitation to wisdom. Chapter 2 discusses the biblical teaching on natural law in more detail.

Natural Law Does Not Confer a Saving Knowledge

One important point that is worth reiterating is that natural law cannot confer a saving knowledge. After the entry of sin into the world, it is not possible to know the truth about God through natural revelation alone, and salvation is not possible through natural law. Due to the "darkness of ignorance and the abyss of sin in which our nature has been immersed," it is not possible to attain a saving knowledge of God through natural law.[18] After the fall of humankind, nature has been corrupted and "no one is able [to] come to true wisdom and blessedness with nature as his guide." It is necessary for God to illuminate our knowledge by his Word and bring us into a saving knowledge of himself.[19]

Conclusion

We can gather the threads of this chapter into a definition of *natural law*.[20] Natural law is the moral order that defines the proper ends of human nature, the good that is to be pursued, and the evil to be avoided. The moral order is partially encapsulated in moral precepts or commands; the Decalogue is a perfect summary of the content of those moral precepts. The work of the moral law is written on the human heart, and our conscience bears witness to it. However, humans suppress that knowledge

18. Franciscus Junius, *The Mosaic Polity*, ed. Andrew M. McGinnis, trans. Todd M. Rester (CLP Academic, 2015), 52.

19. Hemmingsen, *On the Law of Nature*, 22, 74.

20. Useful definitions are also set out in VanDrunen, *Divine Covenants and Moral Order*, 15; Andrew T. Walker, *Faithful Reason: Natural Law Ethics for God's Glory and Our Good* (B&H Academic, 2024), 28–29, 75–76.

in unrighteousness, and our capacity to act in accordance with its precepts is corrupted by sin. As such, natural law is not sufficient for humans to attain salvation, and Scripture is necessary as a clearer statement of the moral law. Finally, laws enacted by civil governments ought to be consistent with the natural law.

This chapter has considered the main elements of the doctrine of natural law. But is this doctrine consistent with the Bible? Chapter 2 considers whether there is scriptural support for these ideas.

2

The Bible and Natural Law

One key question Protestants have relates to the relationship between natural law and the Bible. Is natural law a biblical idea? And why do we need natural law when we have Scripture?

Without attempting to be exhaustive, this chapter explores the extent to which the Bible teaches a principle of natural law.[1] It is true that the Bible does not expressly teach a theory of natural law identical to that of, say, Aquinas. However, the essential natural law concepts of universality, unwrittenness, and the existence of moral norms that are rationally or intuitively discoverable apart from special revelation are found in the Bible.[2]

Universal Knowledge of God Through the Creation

We begin our exploration of what the Bible has to say about natural law by looking at the classic passage Romans 1:18–32.

1. For fuller discussion, readers should consult VanDrunen, *Divine Covenants and Moral Order*.

2. Alan F. Johnson, "Is There a Biblical Warrant for Natural-Law Theories?," *Journal of the Evangelical Theological Society* 25 (1982): 186.

This passage forms part of an extended case that all people are condemned for their sin, which is essential context for Paul's exposition of the gospel in chapter 3 as a righteousness made known apart from the law (3:21). In Romans 1, Paul teaches that God's "invisible attributes, namely, his eternal power and divine nature" are clearly perceived "in the things that have been made," but that such knowledge is suppressed in unrighteousness. For this reason, God's wrath is revealed against the unrighteousness of men (1:19–20). God accordingly gave them over to the lusts of their heart, leading to ever greater sin and perversion (1:24–27).

The classical (and preferable) interpretation of this passage is that Paul teaches "a universal natural knowledge of God and his moral will."[3] What is described in this passage is not ignorance of God and his law but willful suppression of what is known to all people. That is, this passage teaches a universal knowledge of God through the creation.[4]

This is not a complete or saving knowledge, but something that people suppress in unrighteousness. Nevertheless, it provides sufficient knowledge to render all people "without excuse" for their sin and unbelief (1:20).[5] The natural revelation available to all people here serves a negative function, intended to demonstrate that all people, including the gentiles, are justly worthy of condemnation.[6] Romans 1:18–32 alludes to many of the commandments of the Decalogue, including idolatry, disobedience to parents, murder, and sexual sin.[7]

3. VanDrunen, *Divine Covenants and Moral Order*, 212.

4. Some contest this reading of the passage, e.g., Douglas A. Campbell, who argues that Romans 1:19–20 is an "ironic subversion" of the premises of natural revelation. Douglas A. Campbell, "Natural Theology in Paul? Reading Romans 1.19–20," *International Journal of Systematic Theology* 1 (November 1999): 231–52.

5. Douglas J. Moo, *The Epistle to the Romans* (Eerdmans, 1996), 105–8.

6. Charles Hodge, *A Commentary on Romans* (Banner of Truth, 1972), 34.

7. VanDrunen, *Divine Covenants and Moral Order*, 225–26.

Other passages also point to a universal knowledge of God through the creation. "Ask the beasts, and they will teach you; the birds of the heavens, and they will tell you. . . . Who among all these does not know that the hand of the LORD has done this?" (Job 12:7, 9). Psalm 19 teaches that "the heavens declare the glory of God, and the sky above proclaims his handiwork" and that "their voice goes out through all the earth, and their words to the end of the world" (vv. 1–4). Paul and Barnabas told the crowd at Lystra that God "did not leave himself without witness" (Acts 14:15–17). God has left himself a clear testimony in the order and beauty of creation, "from which the reality of the creator God could have been and should have been inferred."[8] God reveals himself through the created order as well as Scripture: God's power and wisdom are truly knowable through "the grandeur and order of nature."[9] All people have "inescapable knowledge of God on the basis of God's self-revelation through nature."[10]

The Law Written on the Heart

Another classic passage on natural law is Romans 2:14–15, which was quoted in chapter 1. This passage teaches that gentiles by nature do what the law requires, even though they do not have the benefit of the written law; this shows that the work of the law is written on their hearts, with their conscience bearing witness to the requirements of the law.

8. James Barr, *Biblical Faith and Natural Theology* (Clarendon Press, 1993), 55; David Haines, *Natural Theology: A Biblical and Historical Introduction and Defense* (Davenant Institute, 2021), 30–31.

9. Steven J. Duby, *God in Himself: Scripture, Metaphysics, and the Task of Christian Theology* (IVP Academic, 2019), 62.

10. Carl F. H. Henry, *God, Revelation, and Authority* (Crossway Books, 1999), 2:130.

One key interpretative question is which "gentiles" are referred to in these verses. Some commentators take the view that Paul is here speaking of gentile Christians, who now have the law written on their hearts.[11] It is beyond the scope of this book to engage in a detailed exegetical analysis of this passage, but the better view is that Paul is speaking of unbelieving gentiles.[12] The purpose of this passage is to demonstrate that God is impartial and just in judging all people for breaching the moral law. How can God justly judge the gentiles who do not have the law? This is only possible if the requirements of the moral law have been revealed to the gentiles in some way, such that they have a knowledge of its requirements.[13]

The text states that *the work of the law* is written on the heart—that is, what the law requires of people,[14] which is referred to in verse 14. The term "by nature" refers to "that which is engraven on our natural constitution," as contrasted with knowledge derived from external sources.[15] All people have sufficient knowledge of the moral law to enable them to distinguish right from wrong. This terminology suggests that the content of natural law is broadly equivalent to the Decalogue, even if not identical.[16]

Thus, Romans 1 and 2 teach that there is an external witness to the existence and character of God through the creation, and an internal witness through the law written on the heart. Through

11. E.g., S. J. Gathercole, "A Law unto Themselves: The Gentiles in Romans 2.14–15 Revisited," *Journal for the Study of the New Testament* 85 (2002): 27–49.

12. Commentators who take this view include Leon Morris, *The Epistle to the Romans* (Eerdmans, 1988), 125; Moo, *The Epistle to the Romans*, 148–51; Herman Ridderbos, *Paul: An Outline of His Theology*, trans. John Richard de Witt (Eerdmans, 1975), 107; John Murray, *The Epistle to the Romans* (Eerdmans, 1968), 72–76; VanDrunen, *Divine Covenants and Moral Order*, 232.

13. VanDrunen, *Divine Covenants and Moral Order*, 235, 245–48.

14. Morris, *The Epistle to the Romans*, 126.

15. Murray, *The Epistle to the Romans*, 73, 75.

16. VanDrunen, *Divine Covenants and Moral Order*, 225, 251, and ch. 7.

general revelation, a nonsalvific knowledge is imparted to all people of a wide range of things, including God's existence, his eternal power and divine nature, human longing for eternal satisfaction, our proclivity to worship, moral obligation, and culpability for breaching that law.[17] As John Calvin writes, "If the Gentiles have the righteousness of the law naturally engraven on their minds, we certainly cannot say that they are altogether blind as to the rule of life. Nothing indeed is more common than for man to be sufficiently instructed in a right course of conduct by natural law, of which the Apostle here speaks."[18]

Created Order in Genesis

The opening chapters of the Bible describe the creation of the world and the embedding of order within that creation. God made the world in six days, forming light, darkness, sky, sea, and land (including vegetation) on the first three days, then filling each of these with sun, moon, stars, living creatures, and humankind on days four to six. The sun and moon were made to separate the day from the night, which are for "signs and for seasons" and "to rule over the day and over the night" (Gen. 1:14–18). In Genesis 1, God "declares that all things were divinely distinguished according to a suitable order, namely day from night, the lower from the higher, and the sea from the dry land."[19]

God made humankind male and female in his image, gave them dominion over the creation and told them to "be fruitful and multiply and fill the earth and subdue it" (Gen. 1:27–28).

17. Walker, *Faithful Reason*, 103–4.

18. John Calvin, *Institutes of the Christian Religion*, ed. John T. McNeill, trans. Ford Lewis Battles (Westminster John Knox, 1960), 2.2.22.

19. Ptolemy of Lucca, *On the Government of Rulers: De Regimine Principum*, trans. James M. Blythe (University of Pennsylvania Press, 1997), 96.

Although different views have been expressed on what precisely the image of God is, a consensus has emerged in Old Testament scholarship that the image of God refers to humanity's office in exercising rule as God's earthly delegates.[20] The image of God "refers to human beings as commissioned with the royal exercise of dominion as God's representatives in this world," exercising kingly rule, rather than any one characteristic such as rationality.[21]

The cycle of work and rest is underscored in the placing of the man in the garden of Eden "to work it and keep it" (Gen. 2:15) and the pattern of the Sabbath day: "On the seventh day God finished his work that he had done, and he rested on the seventh day from all his work that he had done. So God blessed the seventh day and made it holy, because on it God rested from all his work that he had done in creation" (Gen. 2:2–3).

After the creation of man the Lord God said, "It is not good that the man should be alone; I will make him a helper fit for him," and so created the woman (Gen. 2:18, 23–24). This is consistent with the theme of sociability that Christian thinkers have associated with natural law (see chapter 5).

After all things were created, "God saw everything that he had made, and behold, it was very good" (Gen. 1:31). This can be seen as the foundation of the principle of natural law: God made everything "very good." This tells us that the narrative in Genesis is not the mere recording of events or facts with no ongoing significance; rather, it sets out patterns that remain normative. The Decalogue expressly connects the weekly Sabbath with the pattern established at creation (Exod. 20:11). Because God rested on the seventh day, blessed it, and made it holy, this provides the rationale for the weekly rest commanded in the law.

20. J. Richard Middleton, *The Liberating Image: The Imago Dei in Genesis 1* (Brazos Press, 2005), 60.

21. VanDrunen, *Divine Covenants and Moral Order*, 46.

Jesus quoted Genesis 1:27–28 and drew the conclusion that what God has joined together, "let not man separate" (Mark 10:6–9). Because "God made them male and female," certain moral implications follow, including the proper pattern for sex and marital union, reproduction, and the inviolability of marriage. Genesis 1 and 2, therefore, describe a moral order embedded in creation. These facts are not neutral. We are expected to draw "ought" from "is."

Law and Covenant

Having created humans in his image, God imposed a probationary test on Adam, known in the Reformed tradition as the covenant of works. That test included the command not to eat of the tree of the knowledge of good and evil, as well as the moral law written on the heart,[22] and held out the promise of eternal life for obedience and death for disobedience. Although the detailed implications are not spelled out in Scripture, it is likely that the original covenant would not have lasted forever.[23] This suggests that the original state of humankind was geared toward an eschatological goal. Natural law, therefore, was a law directing humans in the task of ruling the world in order to attain the goal of the new creation.[24]

After the fall, the world is beset by sin, conflict, and danger in a way that did not characterize the original creation.[25] The creation has been subjected to futility and longs to be set free

22. The *Westminster Confession of Faith* states that the moral law was given to Adam as a covenant of works: 19.1. Hereafter, references to the *Westminster Confession of Faith* are cited as *WCF*.

23. Geerhardus Vos, *Biblical Theology: Old and New Testaments* (Eerdmans, 1948), 22.

24. VanDrunen, *Divine Covenants and Moral Order*, 33–34, 69–70.

25. VanDrunen, *Divine Covenants and Moral Order*, 119.

from its bondage to corruption (Rom. 8:20–21). It is no longer possible for humans to attain the new creation through obedience to the natural law. One key question that arises from this is the extent to which the original moral order has been marred or lost as a result of the fall.

David VanDrunen has argued that the natural law has been re-articulated and promulgated in the Noahic covenant, which is a universal covenant of preservation under which God governs humanity in its fallen condition.[26] The Noahic covenant reenacts important aspects of the creation order, such as the creation mandate (Gen. 9:1, 6), but in a more muted and pessimistic way (e.g., Gen. 9:2). The Noahic covenant preserves the world and human society, including through human institutions of justice and punishment, mitigating the effects of sin but not promising a final solution to the problem of sin. Under this covenant God continues to make known the moral standards to which all people will be held to account through the natural law, and commissions them "to exercise a modified form of that benevolent dominion over the world to which he originally called them at creation."[27]

According to this account, human participation in the natural law is mediated by covenants and re-articulated within the various covenants that are unfolded throughout the Bible. Given that natural law is refracted through the Noahic covenant, its role has changed, although its fundamental content has not. Because Genesis 9:1–7 is addressed to all humanity, it can be seen as a text "which makes explicit universal knowledge of certain norms," and so is an example of natural law in the Bible.[28]

26. VanDrunen, *Divine Covenants and Moral Order*, ch. 2.

27. VanDrunen, *Divine Covenants and Moral Order*, 209.

28. Jonathan Burnside, *God, Justice, and Society: Aspects of Law and Legality in the Bible* (Oxford University Press, 2011), 79.

Moral Order

The book of Genesis, then, teaches that the universe is not random or purposeless but has been made according to a moral order that is characterized by goodness and harmony.[29] That moral order is built into creation, "inherent in the way things are,"[30] and so is universal, not applying only to God's covenant people. Despite the fall, that moral order continues to be normative in the world and can (at least in principle) be perceived by all people.

Often a sharp contrast is drawn between creation or natural law ethics and redemptive or divine command ethics. However, the Scripture includes both. As well as including divine commands, there is a "creation horizon" to Old Testament ethics; that is, Old Testament thought reflects the view that there is "one comprehensive order of creation" that embraces law, nature, and politics.[31] In Scripture, creation, law, and wisdom texts "share a fundamental belief in a comprehensive ordering of reality," and so biblical law must be seen "within the broader divine purpose for ordered human society."[32] As such, the law is relevant, not just to Israel, but also to the nations.[33]

In the Old Testament, "God and his creation never ultimately speak with two distinct voices"; "all creation expresses God's law and moral purpose, and all God's law is law according to

29. Guenther Haas, "Creational Ethics Is Public Ethics," *Journal for Christian Theological Research* 12 (2007): 6.

30. John Barton, "Natural Law and Poetic Justice in the Old Testament," *Journal of Theological Studies* 30, no. 1 (1979): 5.

31. H. H. Schmid, "Creation, Righteousness and Salvation: 'Creation Theology' as the Broad Horizon of Biblical Theology," in *Creation in the Old Testament*, ed. B. W. Anderson (SPCK; Fortress, 1984), 102–17.

32. Gordon McConville, "Biblical Law and Human Formation," *Political Theology* 14 (2013): 628, 630.

33. Yoram Hazony, *The Philosophy of Hebrew Scripture* (Cambridge University Press, 2012), 346–47.

nature." Thus, both creation and the Torah express God's voice, and the two are fundamentally related.[34]

Psalm 147 draws a parallel between God's word for the creation and God's law for Israel:

> He sends out his word, and melts them;
> he makes his wind blow and the waters flow.
> He declares his word to Jacob,
> his statutes and rules to Israel. (vv. 18–19)

God's word for nature "can be seen as an extension of Torah." The regularities of nature are not independent laws of nature but are the personal work of the Creator.[35]

Many passages of Scripture testify to the existence of a moral order within a creational framework. Psalm 104 emphasizes the "inner harmony of the world," and Psalm 148 portrays many parts of creation praising God.[36] Psalm 19 speaks of a universal testimony to God's glory as Creator, which should drive all people to worship and obedience. The heavenly message proclaimed by God's handiwork "has substantive moral content" because it reveals God's character as the Creator. The linking of biblical law with the testimony of creation suggests that the law is rooted in objective reality, and so is applicable to all people. Natural and divine law speak in harmony.[37] In other passages, the created order

34. Markus Bockmuehl, "Natural Law in Second Temple Judaism," *Vetus Testamentum* 45 (1995): 19–20.

35. Sidney Greidanus, "The Universal Dimension of Law in the Hebrew Scriptures," *Studies in Religion/Sciences Religieuses* 14 (1985): 42.

36. J. G. McConville, *God and Earthly Power: An Old Testament Political Theology* (T&T Clark, 2006), 33.

37. Jonathan Burnside, "Natural Law and Biblical Law," in *Research Handbook on Natural Law Theory*, ed. Jonathan Crowe and Constance Youngwon Lee (Edward Elgar, 2019), 184–88, 191–92.

functions as a witness to biblical law.[38] The works of God's hands and his precepts can be seen in parallel as trustworthy (Ps. 111:7).

The creation of humans in God's image reflects this wise ordering. Several Old Testament texts ground ethical obligation in human nature, such as the prohibition on killing. Murder is wrong because it violates the inherent being of humans created in God's image (see Gen. 9:6).[39] In Job 31:13–15, Job pleads that he has not treated his servants harshly: "Did not he who made me in the womb make him? And did not one fashion us in the womb?" Here Job recognizes an obligation to treat his servant justly, not based on an express biblical commandment, but by virtue of the fact that all people derive their being from the same God.[40] Similar teaching can be found in passages such as Proverbs 14:31, 17:5, and 22:2.

The theme of order is important in the Wisdom Literature, especially the book of Proverbs.[41] Proverbs presents the world as meaningful and orderly, created and ruled by God. It takes as given that humans are able to perceive wisdom by reflecting on that order. God has established "a cosmic order of justice in the creation" that is rooted in God's character and maintained through his righteous rule. The concept of order, which expresses concepts of regularity and continuation and also the moral idea of justice, is central to the biblical understanding of wisdom.[42]

38. E.g., Deut. 4:32; 28:23–24; Job 20:27; Ps. 50:6; 89:6; 119:89; Jer. 2:12.

39. Johnson, "Biblical Warrant," 187.

40. Johnson, "Biblical Warrant," 186–87.

41. Craig G. Bartholomew, "A Time for War, and a Time for Peace: Old Testament Wisdom, Creation and O'Donovan's Theological Ethics," in *A Royal Priesthood? The Use of the Bible Ethically and Politically: A Dialogue with Oliver O'Donovan*, ed. Craig G. Bartholomew, Jonathan Chaplin, Robert Song, and Al Wolters (Zondervan, 2002), 92–93.

42. Leo G. Perdue, *Proverbs* (Westminster John Knox, 2000), 10–11.

The created world is conducive to certain forms of action but not others, and so wisdom is grounded in creation.[43] Consequences both good and ill follow from wise and foolish actions; those who align themselves with God's order will experience good, while fools suffer for their folly.[44] Wisdom involves reflecting on the moral order inherent in creation and living in accordance with that order.[45]

Proverbs charges us to observe the world and draw lessons from it (24:30–32). Those who commit foolish acts are flying in the face of the order inherent in the world. Various proverbs draw parallels between nature and human activity,[46] implying that there are norms that govern both humans and animals.[47] The entire natural order is an interconnected whole.[48] Again, there is a harmony between creation and revelation, which should not surprise us given that God is the author of both.

Passages such as Proverbs 3:19–20 and 8:22–31 have been crucial texts in natural law thinking.[49] Proverbs 3:19–20 declares that "the LORD by wisdom founded the earth; by understanding he established the heavens; by his knowledge the deeps broke open, and the clouds drop down the dew." Consider also Proverbs 8:27–29: "When he established the heavens, I was there; when he drew a circle on the face of the deep, when he made

43. Andrew Errington, *Every Good Path: Wisdom and Practical Reason in Christian Ethics and the Book of Proverbs* (T&T Clark, 2020), 2.

44. Katharine J. Dell, *The Book of Proverbs in Social and Theological Context* (Cambridge University Press, 2006), 134.

45. Leo G. Perdue, "Cosmology and the Social Order in the Wisdom Tradition," in *The Sage in Israel and the Ancient Near East*, ed. John G. Gammie and Leo G. Perdue (Eisenbrauns, 1990), 458–59; Leo G. Perdue, *The Sword and the Stylus: An Introduction to Wisdom in the Age of Empires* (Eerdmans, 2008), 12.

46. Such as Proverbs 30:15–16, 18–19, 24–28, 29–31.

47. John Barton, *Ethics in Ancient Israel* (Oxford University Press, 2014), 112–13, 115.

48. VanDrunen, *Divine Covenants and Moral Order*, 380.

49. Errington, *Every Good Path*, 11.

firm the skies above, when he established the fountains of the deep, when he assigned to the sea its limit, so that the waters might not transgress his command, when he marked out the foundations of the earth." A key theme in both passages is the orderliness of creation: God has created the world and set limits on its functioning, allowing for predictability for people to determine their lives.[50]

Scripture also draws strong parallels between law and wisdom.[51] Deuteronomy presents its laws as the embodiment of wisdom, which could be perceived by the surrounding nations (4:5–8). The law is given in the context of an appeal to Israel to follow God's commandments and not to "turn aside to the right hand or to the left" (5:32). Almost identical language is found in the Wisdom Literature (e.g., Prov. 4:27). Deuteronomy outlines the right path to be taken and the consequences of following different paths (4:1–2; 5:32–33; 28:1–68), which parallels closely the appeals made in the book of Proverbs (e.g., 1:8–33; 2:1–22; 5:1–23).

A legislative model of law often simply mandates or forbids certain conduct on the authority of the lawgiver. A wisdom approach, by contrast, seeks to persuade by its intrinsic merits. The Old Testament includes examples of both models. Some commands are simply given with no explanation or rationale (e.g., Deut. 5:17–21). But many commands come with motives or reasons attached (e.g., Exod. 22:26–27; Deut. 5:6–20; 20:19; 25:3). John Barton argues that even where the ethical teachings of the Old Testament are presented as commands, "there is a surprising weight of material that appeals to reason. Many laws

50. Tomáš Frydrych, *Living Under the Sun: Examination of Proverbs and Qoheleth* (Brill, 2002), 100.

51. David Daube, *Law and Wisdom in the Bible*, ed. Calum Carmichael (Templeton Press, 2010), chaps. 1–3.

come with motive clauses and justifications attached; narratives draw the reader into a moral world in which discrimination is needed; prophetic imperatives form part of a dialogue with a reader or hearer who is supposed to be able to grasp logical consequences of action."[52] The law is given within a broader created order and designed to reflect the inherent rightness of things. Those subject to the law should follow the law, not simply because God has commanded it, but also because it is an inherently wise thing to do.

The prophetic writings give indications that there is a law embodied in creation that humans ought to heed.[53] The book of Isaiah evidences a picture of the world in which God is the Creator and Preserver of everything and acting rightly requires acting consistently with the order that prevails in the creation, which ought to be apparent and which especially includes humility before God.[54] There is a natural order of things, and there are ways of acting that breach this natural order.[55]

Sin is not just a breach of a rule but is unnatural and stupid (e.g., Isa. 1:3; Jer. 8:7). Sin brings destructive consequences (e.g., Prov. 6:27–28; 7:22–27). Denying the existence of God is culpable foolishness (Ps. 14:1). Creating a carved image in order to worship it is an objectively ridiculous thing to do (Isa. 44:18–20). Sin is "a challenge to the natural and true order of things"; it is "cosmic nonsense," an affront to reality.[56] "Do horses run on rocks? Does one plow there with oxen? But you

52. Barton, *Ethics in Ancient Israel*, 274.

53. C. H. Dodd, "Natural Law in the Bible—II," *Theology* 49, no. 312 (1946): 164.

54. John Barton, "Ethics in Isaiah of Jerusalem," *Journal of Theological Studies* 32, no. 1 (1981): 11.

55. John Barton, *Ethics and the Old Testament*, 2nd ed. (SCM Press, 2002), 63, referring to Isa. 1:23; 3:9; 5:8–9, 23; 10:1–2.

56. Barton, "Ethics in Isaiah of Jerusalem," 10; Barton, "Natural Law and Poetic Justice," 7.

have turned justice into poison and the fruit of righteousness into wormwood" (Amos 6:12). Israel's perversion of justice was contrary to nature.[57]

The Bible and the Book of Nature

Sometimes a sharp contrast is drawn between general and special revelation. However, this is not consistent with the Bible's own teaching. While of course special revelation goes well beyond what can be known through nature alone, the teaching of Scripture presupposes the existence of general revelation. The Bible assumes a knowledge of the created order and communicates many truths by employing the categories of natural revelation, such as trees, rocks, breath, flowers, seeds, fruit, animals, and even dung.[58] Scripture does not ignore natural revelation, but its teaching "points readers persistently to the reality of natural revelation. The created order at large is witness to God's creative wisdom, and people should come to share in this wisdom through observing and pondering the ways of the world."[59] The Bible assumes that there are lessons we ought to learn from nature, and God instructs people through natural means (e.g., Isa. 28:23–29).

Many passages of the Bible argue not from what has been expressly revealed but from what is apparent from human nature and society.[60] Many of Jesus's parables draw on experience and things his hearers would have been familiar with, such as the foolishness of building on sand, the sowing of crops,

57. Johnson, "Biblical Warrant," 189.

58. Gerald R. McDermott, *Everyday Glory: The Revelation of God in All of Reality* (Baker Academic, 2018), 54–55, 117.

59. VanDrunen, *Divine Covenants and Moral Order*, 391.

60. Barton, *Ethics and the Old Testament*, 61.

natural phenomena such as trees, wheat, and tares, and leaven's effect on dough (Matt. 7:24–27; 13:1–9, 24–33). Jesus assumed a knowledge of these things drawn from experience.

That is, it could be said that the Bible is not self-contained but depends on a prior knowledge of created reality in order for it to be intelligible.[61] As Francis Turretin wrote, the knowledge of true faith obtainable through special revelation "does not exclude, but supposes the general knowledge from nature."[62]

Universal Moral Law

We have considered how the Bible teaches a broader conception of natural law—namely, a moral order. There is also plenty of support within Scripture for the existence of natural law in its narrower sense mentioned in the previous chapter—namely, a universally applicable moral law, which is knowable imperfectly outside of Scripture.

This goes against the popular belief that biblical morality is the "parade example of a divine command theory"—that is, what is right and wrong is simply what God has commanded.[63] And indeed, it is true that much law in the Old Testament is given specifically to Israel, and the Israelites were to obey the law simply because it was commanded by God.[64] The laws given to Israel were the standards imposed by God, who had personally entered into covenant with his people, and much of the ethical teaching of the Old Testament is particular to Israel.

61. Joe Rigney, "With One Voice: Scripture and Nature for Ethics and Discipleship," *Eikon: A Journal for Biblical Anthropology* 1, no. 1 (Spring 2019): 29.

62. Francis Turretin, *Institutes of Elenctic Theology*, trans. George Musgrave Giger (P&R, 1992), 1:8.

63. Barton, *Ethics in Ancient Israel*, 94.

64. Barton, *Ethics and the Old Testament*, 72.

Yet this leads to a dilemma: The first record of the giving of the written or revealed law is in Exodus 20, in which it was addressed only to Israel. However, there are many passages of Scripture that speak of the existence of right and wrong before the law had been given and use the terminology of *sin* and *evil* in relation to nations to whom the law was not given.[65] The book of Genesis endorses the existence of moral precepts that apply to humanity as a whole.[66] This indicates that the moral law exists and may be known apart from the formal revelation of the written law. Other pre-Decalogue passages clearly invoke the categories of right and wrong and indicate judgment on people for their conduct.[67] In passages such as these, the Old Testament appeals to "self-evident standards of morality."[68]

There is also much universal ethical teaching in the Old Testament. Scripture recognizes that natural law is a standard that all people can recognize (at least in part) but only attain imperfectly; it teaches that there is a "universal knowledge of certain norms."[69] Some peoples, such as Sodom, disregard the moral law in shocking ways, provoking God's judgment (Gen. 19). Others, such as the people of Gerar, show a higher standard of conduct than the covenant people of God (Gen. 20).

Several passages speak of "things that ought not to be done": Genesis 20:9; 34:7; and Romans 1:28. This indicates that there are universal moral boundaries and also that there is some way of knowing these standards outside of the revealed law

65. E.g., Gen. 4:3–12; 6:5–12; 13:13; 18:20–21; 19:1–29; 20:1–18; 34:1–31; 39:6–10.

66. Markus Bockmuehl, "The Noachide Commandments and New Testament Ethics: With Special Reference to Acts 15 and Pauline Halakhah," *Revue Biblique* 102, no. 1 (1995): 81.

67. E.g., Gen. 9:21–27; 11:1–9; 12:10–20; 25:29–34; 26:6–11; 38:24–26; 42:21–28; 44:4–10, 16; Exod. 1:15–21; 2:23–25.

68. Bockmuehl, "Natural Law in Second Temple Judaism," 21.

69. Burnside, *God, Justice, and Society*, 76–77.

in Scripture.[70] Adultery and rape are self-evidently wrong, and all people should know this.[71] The norms in Scripture are often presented as "natural," either because they are shared by right-minded people or because they reflect the inherent nature of things.[72]

There is a universal dimension to the law in Scripture, such that the law is a standard for all people. Israel was to teach the nations as a light for the peoples.[73] Idolatry, conduct in interpersonal relationships, and sexual morality are examples of universal norms based on creation.[74] All people are subject to requirements to honor God alone as Lord,[75] respect human life and show basic humanity to other people,[76] and respect the pattern for marriage and sexuality established at creation.[77]

Deuteronomy contemplates the nations observing Israel in the land, who would be blessed as they followed the Lord's commands (4:1–8). This suggests that the law contains an inherent wisdom and reasonableness that other nations can perceive.

Psalm 119:52 speaks of God's law as "from of old." Commenting on this verse, Calvin noted that the law of God is not of recent growth, "but truly everlasting, because the written law is just an attestation of the law of nature, through means of which God recalls to our memory that which he has previously engraved on our hearts."[78]

70. David VanDrunen, *Natural Law: A Short Companion* (B&H Academic, 2023), ch. 3.

71. Barton, *Ethics in Ancient Israel*, 101.

72. Barton, *Ethics in Ancient Israel*, 102.

73. Isa. 11:9–10, 12; 42:1–4, 6–7; 49:6; 51:4; 60:3; Jer. 3:17; 4:1–2.

74. Greidanus, "Universal Dimension of Law," 43–48.

75. E.g., Gen. 11; Isa. 10:12–13; 14:22–23; Dan. 4:27–37.

76. E.g., Gen. 9:5–6; Job 31:13–15; Dan. 4:27; Amos 1:2–2:3.

77. E.g., Gen. 1:28; 20:3–4; Lev. 18:24–25.

78. John Calvin, *Commentary on the Book of Psalms*, vol. 4, trans. James Anderson (Baker, 2003), 438. Calvin went on to say: "I am rather inclined to

Assumed Moral Principles

There are several passages in Scripture in which moral principles are assumed rather than stated. These include the following.

Proportionate punishment. In Genesis 18, in view of the impending judgment on Sodom, Abraham pleads with God not to put the righteous to death with the wicked: "Far be that from you! Shall not the Judge of all the earth do what is just?" (v. 25). Abraham here recognizes the principle that people should be punished for their own sins, not the sins of others, and that it is wrong to impose punishment on the innocent.

This seems to set up a standard by which to judge God's actions.[79] What is interesting from a natural law perspective is that there is no record in Scripture of this principle having been revealed to Abraham prior to this.[80] That is, Abraham's plea indicates an awareness of a principle that was recognized as self-evidently true, and that created a problem because God's actions were perceived to be inconsistent with that standard. A similar principle is also recognized in Ezekiel 18.

Gratitude. Fundamental to much of the ethical teaching of the Old Testament is the principle of obedience flowing from gratitude (e.g., Exod. 20:2). But the Old Testament does not spell out why this should be the case, assuming rather that it is self-evident.[81]

Provision for one's family. Paul wrote to Timothy that "if anyone does not provide for his relatives, and especially for

---

adopt another interpretation, That David remembered the judgments of God, by which he testified that he had established his law perpetually in the world."

79. See C. S. Rodd, "Shall Not the Judge of All the Earth Do What Is Just? (Gen. 18:25)," *Expository Times* 83 (1972): 137–39.

80. See also Jer. 31:29–33; Ezek. 18:1–4, 25–32.

81. Barton, *Ethics and the Old Testament*, 90–92.

members of his household, he has denied the faith and is worse than an unbeliever" (1 Tim. 5:8). That people should provide for their family is a self-evident obligation that should be recognized by all people.

Judgment on the Nations

There are many passages of Scripture that condemn people for their sins or record judgment on the nations, including non-Israelite people and nations.[82] This includes the judgment on the world leading to the flood, the scattering of the nations at Babel, judgment on Sodom and Gomorrah (Gen. 6:5–8; 11:1–9; 19), the destruction of the Canaanite nations (Josh. 6; 8; 10; 11), and prophetic denunciation of pagan nations.[83] The New Testament contains similar warnings of judgment (2 Cor. 5:10; Gal. 5:19–21; Col. 3:5–7).

It would be unreasonable to condemn someone for breaching a standard that does not apply to them and of which they have no knowledge. Consistent with this, the nations are never judged on the basis of their failure to keep the law revealed to Israel. The imposition of judgment on people who are outside the covenant community therefore entails that there is a moral law applicable to those nations and that they have some awareness of that standard (natural law in the narrow sense). These judgments are a reminder that all people know the fundamentals of the moral law and that all people are accountable to God for their violation.[84]

82. E.g., Gen. 13:13; 15:16; 19:1–29; Deut. 7:1–16; 9:4–5; 12:1–3; Josh. 6; 8; 10; 11; 2 Kings 16:3; 21:2; Isa. 13–23; Jer. 46–51; Ezek. 25–32; 35; 38–39; Dan. 4; 5; Amos 1:3–2:3; Zeph. 2; and the books of Obadiah, Jonah, and Nahum.

83. Isa. 13–23; Jer. 46–51; Ezek. 25–30; 35; 38–39; Dan. 4; 5; Amos 1–2.

84. VanDrunen, *Divine Covenants and Moral Order*, 137–38, 165.

Amos 1–2 is an important text relating to natural law. Amos records judgment on the nations surrounding Israel for what may broadly be described as brutal treatment of other peoples, and then homes in on Judah and Israel. There is an important contrast between the standard applied to the nations and that which is applied to Judah and Israel: The nations are judged for their brutality and inhumanity, but the people of Judah are judged "because they have rejected the law of the LORD" (Amos 2:4). Thus, in this passage the prophet does not appeal to the written law in relation to the nations, but to standards of morality that are applicable and knowable outside the law.[85] This suggests that Amos recognizes the existence of universal and self-evident moral norms.[86] The conduct of the nations was so inhumane that they ought to have known it was evil, and so God is just for judging them for breaching a standard they ought to have known.[87] Amos provides biblical support for the idea that there exist self-evident principles of morality.

In his speech to the Areopagus, Paul, noting the idolatry of the Athenians, told his listeners that "the times of ignorance God overlooked, but now he commands all people everywhere to repent, because he has fixed a day on which he will judge the world in righteousness" (Acts 17:30–31). As put by James Barr, "Idolatry is wrong because it puts the created in the place of the creator; it venerates that which God has made instead of venerating the God who made it."[88]

85. Barton, *Ethics in Ancient Israel*, 101; Barton, *Ethics and the Old Testament*, 62–63.

86. John Barton, *The Theology of the Book of Amos* (Cambridge University Press, 2012), 59; Graham R. Hamborg, *Hosea, Joel, and Amos* (Cambridge University Press, 2023), 282.

87. Paul Noble, "Israel Among the Nations," *Horizons in Biblical Theology* 15 (1993): 65.

88. Barr, *Biblical Faith and Natural Theology*, 65.

Unbelievers Can Perceive Wisdom and the Moral Law

Scripture recognizes that wisdom is not the preserve of believers only, but those outside the covenant community can grasp it. Unbelievers can understand the wisdom of the law and the rightness of living in accordance with God's commands.[89] This suggests that the law is not simply an arbitrary set of commands but that there is an inherent wisdom to God's law and that by being made in God's image humans are able to perceive that reasonableness (see also 1 Kings 4:34; 10:6–9). Genuine wisdom exists among the non-covenant nations (Jer. 49:7; Ezek. 28:12; Obad. 8).

Some passages of Scripture depict unbelievers as adhering to a higher standard of conduct than God's own people.[90] Genesis 20, where Abraham deceives and is rebuked by Abimelech, a king outside the covenant community, is an excellent example of this. This text functions "with a sense of natural law as a part of the created order of things that can be discerned and observed apart from faith."[91] In 1 Corinthians 5, Paul chastises the Corinthian church for permitting sexual immorality, noting that such conduct would not be tolerated among pagans (v. 1). Unbelievers, therefore, can act to a higher standard than those within the covenant community (see also Ezek. 5:6–8).

The New Testament and Natural Law

So far we have explored passages from the Old Testament as well as the important New Testament passages Romans 1:18–32

89. Deut. 4:5–8; 1 Thess. 4:12; 1 Pet. 2:12.

90. C. John Collins, "Echoes of Aristotle in Romans 2:14–15: Or, Maybe Abimelech Was Not So Bad After All," *Journal of Markets & Morality* 13, no. 1 (Spring 2010): 123, 141–42.

91. Terrence E. Fretheim, *The Book of Genesis* (Abingdon, 1994), 483.

and 2:14–15 that teach a doctrine of natural law. But does Jesus teach a doctrine of natural law? Christ's radical kingdom ethic of self-denial is sometimes thought to be at odds with a universally accessible moral law.

The New Testament teaches that all things have been made through Christ, who upholds all things by his powerful word (John 1:3; Col. 1:16–17; Heb. 1:3). If the world has been made according to an order, then it follows that Christ himself established and upholds the moral order that characterizes creation. In many ways, Christ's teaching in the Gospels is consistent with the principle of natural law, often being based on or drawing from ordinary experiences. He assumes that his hearers have an understanding of ordinary life, including shared standards of conduct. Jesus repeatedly appeals to a human consensus about what is just and unjust, a consensus that is not derived solely from written revelation but rests on ideas that are formed by reflection on human nature and human social life. This is very consistent with natural law thinking.[92]

Jesus appeals to a universal reality of parental generosity to illustrate God's kindness to his children (Matt. 7:9–12). He affirms important aspects of the created moral order, including the normative pattern of the original creation order. When asked whether divorce is permissible, Jesus appeals to the creation of humans as male and female to conclude that divorce is contrary to that order (19:4–9).

Jesus's parables often draw from everyday realities that would be known to his hearers and assume the existence of accepted standards of judgment and behavior.[93] The parable of the two sons reflects the widely held belief that one should follow

92. Johnson, "Biblical Warrant," 194.
93. Dodd, "Natural Law," 162.

through on one's commitments (21:28–32). In the parable of the unforgiving servant, Jesus's hearers would have recognized that it would be wrong for a man to insist on the repayment of a pittance when he has been forgiven a vast sum (18:21–35). In the parable of the workers in the vineyard, the owner states: "Am I not allowed to do what I choose with what belongs to me?" (20:15). The point would be lost without a common agreement that the owner may dispose of his wealth as he sees fit and be recognized to be just in so doing.[94]

Before healing the man with the withered hand, Jesus says to those who seek to accuse him: "Is it lawful on the Sabbath to do good or to do harm, to save life or to kill?" (Mark 3:4; see also Matt. 12:11–12). Jesus here appeals to his hearers' innate "moral sense of the difference between good and harm" even though there is no commandment in the Torah that permits healing on the Sabbath.[95]

The New Testament affirms the natural moral order and requires Christians to honor institutions that support that order such as marriage, family, and civil government. Unbelieving civil rulers are described as servants of God "for your good," whose role is to "punish those who do evil and to praise those who do good" (Rom. 13:1–7; 1 Pet. 2:13–17). This implies that those rulers have some capacity to determine what is good and evil and enforce punishment against those who breach that standard.

Conclusion

How can we sum up the relationship between the Bible and natural law? First, the Bible gives certainty and a much clearer

94. Johnson, "Biblical Warrant," 193.
95. Johnson, "Biblical Warrant," 191.

and more authoritative statement of the moral law.[96] Our natural knowledge of the moral law is liable to be corrupted, and that distorted knowledge needs to be corrected. John Calvin likened the Scripture to spectacles that correct our defective knowledge of God through natural revelation.[97]

Second, the Bible instructs in supernatural matters that could not otherwise be known.[98] Apart from Scripture, we could not know the truth of the Trinity or the due manner of worshiping God, or ascertain the means of salvation; these are things that need to be specifically revealed to us.[99]

Third, the Bible assumes some natural law principles without restating them.[100] One example, mentioned earlier in this chapter, is the principle of gratitude. The prologue to the Decalogue states: "I am the Lord your God, who brought you out of the land of Egypt, out of the house of slavery" (Exod. 20:2). This makes sense because "God has implanted a law concerning gratitude in the minds of men."[101]

Finally, the Bible contains determinations or applications of the natural law. Writers in the Christian tradition have described the laws of Moses as an application of the natural law to the people of Israel.[102] It is not the laws of Moses that are binding on all people at all times but only the moral principles they give

96. J. Budziszewski, *Commentary on Thomas Aquinas's Treatise on Divine Law* (Cambridge University Press, 2021), 10.

97. Calvin, *Institutes of the Christian Religion*, 1.6.1.

98. Budziszewski, *Treatise on Divine Law*, 8, 10, 53.

99. Richard Hooker, *Of the Laws of Ecclesiastical Polity: A Critical Edition with Modern Spelling*, ed. Arthur Stephen McGrade (Oxford University Press, 2013), 1:85 [1.11.5–6]; 1:90–91 [1.14.1].

100. Budziszewski, *Treatise on Divine Law*, 19.

101. Hemmingsen, *On the Law of Nature*, 116–17; J. Budziszewski, *Commentary on Thomas Aquinas's Treatise on Law* (Cambridge University Press, 2014), 275.

102. Some laws (e.g., food laws) are not generally considered to be an application of natural law principles.

effect to. Natural law, then, functions as an important tool for interpreting Scripture, helping us to discern how the Mosaic laws apply today.[103]

As stated at the start of this chapter, there has often been resistance to the idea that the Bible teaches natural law.[104] There is increasing recognition that this is at odds with what the Bible actually teaches and that creation and moral order are not peripheral themes.[105]

What the Bible teaches is not exactly the same as scholastic or contemporary theories of natural law. But I have argued in this chapter that the Bible teaches the main elements of the principle of natural law—namely, that there is a moral order in creation (the broader sense of natural law) and a universally applicable moral law (the narrow sense of natural law) and that these are knowable by all people (although imperfectly) outside of Scripture.

103. Junius, *Mosaic Polity*, 8, 11, 60, 62.
104. Barton, *Ethics in Ancient Israel*, 95–96.
105. Schmid, "Creation, Righteousness and Salvation."

3

The Content of Natural Law

Even those who are convinced from the previous chapter that the Bible teaches natural law may still be wondering whether natural law posits the existence of moral principles that are not contained in Scripture. In other words, what precisely is the content of natural law? This chapter explores the content of natural law, comparing the Bible's teaching about the moral law with traditional Christian accounts of the content of natural law.

Within the Christian tradition (both Roman Catholic and Protestant), there have been three main ways of defining the content of the natural law. Christian thinkers have argued that natural law consists of a series of primary precepts, that natural law is equivalent to the Golden Rule, and that natural law is summarized in the Decalogue. More recent writers have argued for a fourth: that natural law consists of several self-evident goods. We will look at each of these in turn.[1] The existence of

1. Another possible category, which I do not consider here, is the Jewish doctrine of the Noahide laws: see David Novak, *Natural Law in Judaism* (Cambridge University Press, 1998), 149–50.

these diverse ways of defining the natural law also provokes an interesting question: Can they be harmonized?

I also tackle the controversial question of whether Protestants can recognize the existence of moral precepts that are not directly taught in the Bible but ought to be considered as normative. I suggest that, although caution is warranted, there are some moral principles that should be accepted.

The Primary Precepts of Natural Law

First, many writers have considered that the natural law consists of a series of primary precepts defined by reference to human nature. The following passage from Thomas Aquinas is the canonical exposition of the content of natural law:

> Since, however, good has the character of an end and evil is its opposite, it follows that all those things to which man has a natural inclination are naturally apprehended by reason as being good, and consequently as things to be pursued, and their opposites as evil, and as objects to be avoided. The order of the precepts of the natural law is therefore according to the order of our natural inclinations. For in man there is, first, an inclination to a good according to the nature which he has in common with all substances: that is, inasmuch as every substance seeks the preservation of its own being according to its nature; and, according to this inclination, whatever is a means of preserving human life belongs to the natural law, and whatever impedes it is contrary to it. Second, there is in man an inclination to certain more specific ends which he has by nature in common with other animals; and, according to this inclination, "those things which nature has taught to all animals" are said to belong to the natural law, such as the union of male and female and the education of the young and similar things. Third, there is

> in man an inclination to a good specific to himself, belonging to his rational nature. Thus man has a natural inclination to know the truth concerning God and to live in society; and, accordingly, whatever pertains to this inclination belongs to the natural law: for instance, to shun ignorance, to avoid giving offence to those among whom one has to live, and other such things. (*ST* I-II, 94.2)

According to Aquinas, natural law consists of precepts that can be organized into three categories: precepts pertaining to all things (precept 1), precepts pertaining to living creatures (precepts 2 and 3), and precepts pertaining specifically to humans (precepts 4 and 5).[2] The precepts listed by Aquinas are intended to be illustrative and not exhaustive, and Aquinas considered that the natural law contains other precepts.[3] Nevertheless, writers have often distilled five core primary precepts of the natural law from this passage:

(1) The preservation of life: Whatever is a means of preserving human life belongs to the natural law, and whatever impedes it is contrary to it.
(2) Reproduction, including the union of male and female.
(3) The education of the young.
(4) Living in society, which includes avoiding giving offense to those among whom one has to live.
(5) Worship of God: Man has a natural inclination to know the truth concerning God.[4]

2. John Finnis argues that this threefold order "should be set aside as an irrelevant schematization": *Natural Law and Natural Rights*, 95.

3. Steven J. Jensen, *Knowing the Natural Law: From Precepts and Inclinations to Deriving Oughts* (Catholic University of America Press, 2015), 42.

4. See also Charles E. Rice, *Fifty Questions on the Natural Law* (Ignatius Press, 1999), 52.

This chapter will discuss the nature of these precepts in more detail. Writers in the Protestant tradition have taken a similar view of the natural law, considering (like Aquinas) that the natural law falls into three categories—namely, precepts pertaining to all things, precepts pertaining to living creatures, and precepts pertaining to humans. For example, Girolamo Zanchi wrote that the content of natural law is as follows:

> First, people can protect themselves against any violence or injury. This is a natural reaction for all things. Even trees and plants protect themselves from harm as much as they can. From this instinct comes the idea included in the laws of nations that it is permitted to repel force with force.
>
> Second, human beings can protect not only themselves but also advance their race through the procreation and education of children. This we have also in common with the animals. Because of this impulse, civil lawyers include marriage, reproduction, and rearing children under natural law.
>
> Third, an idea appropriate more for humans than for animals, human beings must recognize their inclination to God and worship him as they do good to those with whom they live, and they must know justice and honesty and turn to them naturally.[5]

It can be seen how closely this mirrors Aquinas's exposition. Protestant writers George Gillespie and Franciscus Junius defined the natural law in very similar terms.[6] It has therefore been common for the Christian tradition to define the natural law as consisting of five primary precepts falling into three categories.

5. Zanchi, *On the Law in General*, 10–11; see also 19.

6. George Gillespie, *A Dispute Against the English-Popish Ceremonies Obtruded on the Church of Scotland*, ed. Chris Coldwell (Naphtali Press, 2013), 361–62; Junius, *Mosaic Polity*, 45–46.

Natural Law and the Golden Rule

Many writers in the Christian tradition have considered that the Golden Rule is a summary expression of the natural law. Gratian's *Decretum*, a highly influential medieval compilation of canon law texts, defines *natural law* as follows: "Natural law is what is contained in the Law and the Gospel. By it, each person is commanded to do to others what he wants done to himself and prohibited from inflicting on others what he does not want done to himself. So Christ said in the Gospel 'Whatever you want men to do to you, do so to them. This indeed is the Law and the Prophets.'"[7]

This was a frequent theme of Martin Luther's writings, for example: "Christ himself (Matt. 7[:12]) includes all of the law and the prophets in this natural law, 'So whatever you wish that men would do to you, do so to them; for this is the law and the prophets.'"[8] George Gillespie agreed that "the law of nature bids us do to others as we would have others to do unto us."[9] Niels Hemmingsen wrote that "it is the justice of nature that no one does to another what he does not wish to be done to himself."[10] Zanchi also saw the Golden Rule as a restatement of the natural law.[11]

7. Gratian, *The Treatise on Laws with the Ordinary Gloss*, trans. Augustine Thompson and James Gordley (Catholic University of America Press, 1993), D.1. This was quoted approvingly by Thomas Aquinas: *ST* I-II, 94.4.

8. Martin Luther, "Against the Heavenly Prophets in the Matter of Images and Sacraments," trans. Bernhard Erling and Conrad Bergendoff, in *Selected Writings of Martin Luther: 1523–1526*, ed. Theodore G. Tappert (Fortress Press, 2007), 175; also the treatises "Whether Soldiers, Too, Can Be Saved" and "Trade and Usury," in the same volume, at pp. 87, 454; Martin Luther, "Temporal Authority: To What Extent It Should Be Obeyed," in *Selected Writings of Martin Luther: 1520–1523*, ed. Theodore G. Tappert (Fortress Press, 2007), 317–18.

9. Gillespie, *English-Popish Ceremonies*, 362.

10. Hemmingsen, *On the Law of Nature*, 97, 100.

11. Zanchi, *On the Law in General*, 20.

The Golden Rule is often considered to be closely related to the fourth precept of the natural law, relating to sociability, and necessary to give effect to that precept. That is, in order to live peaceably in society, we should avoid giving offense and so do to others as we would have done to us.[12]

Natural Law and the Decalogue

Third, Christian thinkers have often argued that the Ten Commandments are a renewed statement of the natural law, and so the natural law is broadly equivalent in content to the Decalogue, although not identical. Gillespie wrote that "if we consider what law was written in the nature of man in his first creation, it was no other than the decalogue, or the moral law," thus treating the moral law, the natural law, and the Decalogue as synonymous.[13] Luther wrote that the Ten Commandments "are not Mosaic laws only, but also the natural law written in each man's heart, as St. Paul teaches (Rom. 2[:15])."[14] Hemmingsen considered that "the law of God, which we customarily call the Decalogue, is said to be a summary of the law of nature."[15] Lutheran theologian Johann Gerhard argues that the Decalogue is a repetition of the law that was originally engrafted onto people's minds, given as a clear statement of the law "to repair the defectiveness of our natural light."[16]

12. Zanchi, *On the Law in General*, 20; Gillespie, *English-Popish Ceremonies*, 362.

13. Gillespie, *English-Popish Ceremonies*, 359. See also George Gillespie, *Aaron's Rod Blossoming; or The Divine Ordinance of Church Government Vindicated* (Sprinkle Publications, 1985 [1646]), 121.

14. See Luther, "Against the Heavenly Prophets," 175–76.

15. Hemmingsen, *On the Law of Nature*, 90.

16. Johann Gerhard, *On the Law*, ed. Benjamin T. G. Mayes and Joshua J. Hayes, trans. Richard J. Dinda (Concordia Publishing House, 2015 [1613]), 24, 28, 166.

Zanchi wrote that "because the Decalogue defines and describes the same things that are called natural law, the Ten Commandments themselves are often called 'natural law.'"[17] This explains why all people are subject to the Ten Commandments even though they were revealed only to Israel; as Althusius said, "The Decalogue has been prescribed for all people to the extent that it agrees with and explains the common law of nature for all peoples."[18] Zacharias Ursinus, principal author of the *Heidelberg Catechism*, wrote that the natural law was written on the heart of humankind at creation and subsequently repeated in the Decalogue due to the obscuring of its knowledge by sin. "The Decalogue is, therefore, the renewal and re-enforcing of the natural law, which is only a part of the Decalogue."[19]

Natural Law as Self-Evident Goods

A recent school of thought, known as the new natural law theory, has sought to define natural law as a series of self-evident and noninstrumental goods. These are the foundational principles of morality that cannot be proven from other principles, and they are good in and of themselves and not means to other ends (these concepts are explained further in chapter 5). John Finnis, an influential new natural law theorist, defined the basic forms of good as life (including health and procreation), knowledge, play, beauty or aesthetic experience, friendship and sociability, practical reasonableness (i.e., living

17. Zanchi, *On the Law in General*, 24.

18. Johannes Althusius, *Politica: An Abridged Translation of Politics Methodically Set Forth and Illustrated with Sacred and Profane Examples*, ed. and trans. Frederick S. Carney (Liberty Fund, 1995), 144 [21.29].

19. Zacharias Ursinus, *Commentary on the Heidelberg Catechism*, trans. G. W. Williard (T. P. Bucher, 1852), 492.

according to a rational plan for life, which includes freedom, reason, integrity and authenticity), and religion.[20] Other goods include family, justice, vocation, skillfulness, authenticity, and pleasure, although some consider these to be subsumed within other categories.[21]

Reconciling Natural Law and the Bible

We have just considered four ways of defining the content of the natural law. One apparent difficulty is that the Decalogue and the natural law seem very different in content. The standard view of the Christian tradition is that the moral law is perfectly summarized by the Decalogue and that natural law and the Decalogue are both statements of the moral law; as such, they teach essentially the same content. However, the canonical expositions of natural law at face value appear to be very different from the Decalogue. Consider the Decalogue set alongside the primary precepts of the natural law on the following page.

The Ten Commandments are clear, precise, theocentric, authoritative, and convicting. The precepts of the natural law, by contrast, can strike us as vague, unclear, and anthropocentric. How can these statements be considered summaries of the same moral law? How might we reconcile the Decalogue with

20. Finnis, *Natural Law and Natural Rights*, 86–90. See also Walker, *Faithful Reason*, 163–65, listing life (including health), family, friendship, knowledge, aesthetic appreciation (beauty), practical reasonableness, integrity, religion, and play; Jonathan Crowe, *Natural Law and the Nature of Law* (Cambridge University Press, 2019), 35 ("life, health, pleasure, friendship, play, appreciation, understanding, meaning and reasonableness").

21. For further discussion, see Germain Grisez, *The Way of the Lord Jesus: Christian Moral Principles* (Franciscan Press, 1997), 121–25; Alfonso Gómez-Lobo, *Morality and the Human Goods* (Georgetown University Press, 2002), ch. 2; Mark C. Murphy, *Natural Law and Practical Rationality* (Cambridge University Press, 2001), ch. 3; Sophie Grace Chappell, *Understanding Human Goods* (Edinburgh University Press, 1998), 37–45.

TEN COMMANDMENTS: DEUTERONOMY 5:7–21	**THE PRECEPTS OF THE NATURAL LAW***
You shall have no other gods before me.	The first precept of the law of nature [is] that man should seek his own conservation, and avoid his own destruction.
You shall not make for yourself a carved image, or any likeness of anything that is in heaven above, or that is on the earth beneath, or that is in the water under the earth. You shall not bow down to them or serve them. . . .	Secondly, as man is a living creature, the law of nature teaches him to propagate and conserve his kind. Whereupon these conclusions do follow, *viz.*, the commixtion [*union*] of male and female, the procreation of children, the educating of them, and providing for them.
You shall not take the name of the Lord your God in vain, for the Lord will not hold him guiltless who takes his name in vain.	The law of nature teaches man to know that there is a God, and that this God is to be worshiped; whereupon it follows that man should seek to know God, and the manner of His worship.
Observe the Sabbath day, to keep it holy, as the Lord your God commanded you. Six days you shall labor and do all your work, but the seventh day is a Sabbath to the Lord your God. . . .	The law of nature teaches man to hold fast friendship and amity with his neighbors . . . [and] bids us do to others as we would have others to do unto us. . . . It follows, that we should not offend other men; that we should keep promises; stand to bargains; give to every man his own.
Honor your father and your mother. . . .	As touching a man's self, the law of nature teaches him . . . that he should live honestly and virtuously, that he should observe order and decency in all his actions.
You shall not murder.	
You shall not commit adultery.	
You shall not steal.	
You shall not bear false witness against your neighbor.	
You shall not covet your neighbor's wife . . . or anything that is your neighbor's.	

* This is drawn from Gillespie's exposition of natural law in *English-Popish Ceremonies*, 361–62.

what Christian thinkers have considered to be the content of the natural law? I argue that they can be seen as mutually illuminating articulations of the moral law whereby the precepts of the natural law correspond to (but are not identical to) the commandments of the Decalogue.

The Decalogue has traditionally been divided into two tables: The first four commandments express the way in which we show love for God, and the last six commandments express the way in which we show love for our neighbor. The precepts of the natural law correspond to both tables. That is, the first four precepts (the preservation of life, reproduction, the education of the young, and living in society) correspond to the second table of the Decalogue, and the fifth precept (worship of God) corresponds to the first table of the Decalogue.

Let us look more closely at each precept of the natural law and its connection to the Decalogue.

The preservation of life. Aquinas's first precept, the preservation of life, clearly corresponds to the sixth commandment ("you shall not murder"), reflecting the fact that humans are created in God's image. The commandment and the natural inclination are two sides of the coin: We are commanded not to murder because life is precious, and likewise we have an inbuilt inclination to preserve life because we recognize the reality that life is precious. In this way precept and human nature mutually reflect and reinforce each other.

Reproduction and the union of male and female. Aquinas's second precept corresponds to the fifth ("honor your father and your mother") and seventh commandments ("you shall not commit adultery"). There is a natural human inclination to desire sexual union and to marry, and "the honorable and lawful bond of spouses is the seedbed of human society."[22] The seventh commandment is intended to harness sexual union within a marriage covenant, which provides a stable context for the raising of children. Again, the commandment and human inclinations mutually reflect each other.

The education of the young. The education of the young (Aquinas's third precept) corresponds to the fifth commandment. While the fifth commandment is directed at children, it has traditionally been understood as also imposing duties on parents.[23] The commandment reflects a broader principle that

22. Hemmingsen, *On the Law of Nature*, 95.
23. As reflected in passages such as Eph. 6:4; Col. 3:21; 1 Tim. 5:8.

God has established families as the rightful context for the raising of children and has implanted mutual feelings of care, love, and tenderness within family relationships.

Unlike many animals, human children are born helpless, unable to do even the most basic of tasks for themselves; children need protection, nurture, and instruction from parents and others. This imposes duties on both parents and children toward each other. Sixteenth-century Reformer Heinrich Bullinger argued that parents have a duty to nourish and feed their children, to teach and instruct them in the substance of the Christian faith, and to find them a suitable occupation.[24] Aquinas's third precept and the fifth commandment correspond to each other and reflect this order implanted within creation.[25] Indeed, Reformed writers thought that the natural law helps us to properly interpret the fifth commandment.[26]

Living in society. Aquinas's fourth precept is that people have a natural inclination to live in society, and, accordingly, "whatever pertains to this inclination belongs to the natural law," such as avoiding giving offense to those among whom one has to live (*ST* I-II, 94.2). Similarly, Gillespie writes, "The law of nature teaches man to hold fast friendship and amity with his neighbors, forasmuch as he is *animal sociale* [social animal]. . . . For the law of nature bids us do to others as we would have others to do unto us (Luke 6:31). And from these precepts it follows, that we should not offend other men; that we should keep promises; stand to bargains; give to every man his own, etc."[27] That is, Gillespie considered that the principle

24. Heinrich Bullinger, *The Decades of Henry Bullinger*, ed. Thomas Harding (Reformation Heritage Books, 2004), 1:291–94.

25. See further Hemmingsen, *On the Law of Nature*, 78.

26. E.g., John Calvin, *Commentaries on the Last Four Books of Moses*, trans. Charles Bingham (Baker Books, 2003), 3:11–12.

27. Gillespie, *English-Popish Ceremonies*, 362.

of human sociability encompasses a range of more specific precepts including rendering justice to others and keeping promises.[28] Thinkers such as Aquinas also considered that man is "a social and political animal."[29] That is, it is an inherent feature of human nature to form communities, and also legal and political structures to govern those communities.

There is plenty of scriptural evidence that humans are made for fellowship and community with others. God made a helper fit for Adam because it was "not good that the man should be alone" (Gen. 2:18). Proverbs states that "whoever isolates himself seeks his own desire; he breaks out against all sound judgment" (18:1). Christians are commanded not to neglect meeting together, but to encourage one another (Heb. 10:25). It seems to be an inherent feature of human nature that we are built for community.

Each of the commandments of the second table of the Decalogue can be seen to correspond with this precept of the natural law, relating to living in society and not giving offense. That is, if we would live peaceably in society, we must do the following: respect authority (consistent with the fifth commandment); not harm or endanger the lives of others (consistent with the sixth commandment); respect other people's marriages (consistent with the seventh commandment); respect other people's property (consistent with the eighth commandment); not tell falsehoods about other people (consistent with the ninth commandment); and not covet what belongs to others (consistent with the tenth commandment).

In all these ways we should do to others as we would have done to us, as the Golden Rule stipulates. The commandments

28. See also Hemmingsen, *On the Law of Nature*, 93–100.

29. Thomas Aquinas, *On Kingship, to the King of Cyprus*, trans. Gerald B. Phelan (Pontifical Institute of Mediaeval Studies, 1949), 4.

of the second table set out specific requirements that reflect a broader principle of human sociability.

Therefore, the first four precepts of the natural law correspond to the commandments of the second table of the Decalogue. Chapter 1 argued that natural law is the biblical teaching that there is a moral order inscribed in creation and that the precepts of the moral law are one important part of this order. The specific commands set out in the Decalogue are consistent with aspects of our created nature, and the inclinations that are proper to that nature. In this way, "law" (the precepts of the moral law) and "nature" (the created order) correspond to each other and can be seen as complementary ways of expressing similar truths.

Worship of God. The fifth precept of the natural law is that humans have a natural inclination to know the truth concerning God and render due worship to him. The first four commandments correspond to this inclination. The law of nature requires that we worship the one true God; the first table of the Decalogue requires that God must be worshiped with mind and heart, according to the first commandment, in the manner specified by God himself, according to the second, and with the mouth and tongue, according to the third.[30]

Note that the claim is not that the natural law is sufficient to give a full understanding of God and the proper manner in which he is to be worshiped. Rather, the claim is that, as Gillespie writes, "the law of nature teaches man to know that there is a God, and that this God is to be worshiped; whereupon it follows, that man should seek to know God and the manner of his worship."[31] That is, the creation provides "an evident

30. Hemmingsen, *On the Law of Nature*, 91.
31. Gillespie, *English-Popish Ceremonies*, 362.

and immovable testimony which shows that God exists and of what sort He is and that He judges,"[32] and this testimony should impel us to obtain a fuller knowledge of this Creator, which is revealed more clearly in Scripture.

There are Scripture texts that speak of unbelievers having the fear of God (e.g., Gen. 20:8–11; Exod. 1:18–21). This is probably not referring to a covenant relationship with God, but rather to pagan kings, not illumined by Scripture, having some measure of respect for the universal norms of creation.[33] Thus, as was stated earlier in chapter 2, there is evidence in Scripture for the existence of a nonsaving knowledge of God and his law.

This reflects the biblical teaching that something of God's character is revealed in creation and that humans "should seek God, and perhaps feel their way toward him and find him" (Acts 17:27; Rom. 1:19–20).[34] Scripture is of course necessary to attain a full and saving knowledge of God and the manner of his due worship. Not all the commands of the first table of the Decalogue are contained in the natural law in the sense that they could be deduced by reason alone; they are matters that need to be revealed to us in Scripture.[35] Scripture and the Decalogue contain a much clearer specification of the moral law, revealing more authoritatively who God is and how he is to be worshiped.

This precept of natural law is also relevant to the fourth commandment. The *Westminster Confession of Faith* states that "it is the law of nature, that, in general, a due proportion of time be set apart for the worship of God" (*WCF* 21.7). That is, it is a requirement of natural law that humans should set aside time

32. Melanchthon, *Chief Theological Topics*, 504.
33. VanDrunen, *Divine Covenants and Moral Order*, 160, 197, 204.
34. See Barr, *Biblical Faith and Natural Theology*, 24–26, 34.
35. Aquinas, *ST* I-II, 100.1; Budziszewski, *Treatise on Divine Law*, 20.

for rest and worship, and apart from Scripture it is possible to deduce an obligation to worship the Creator. But the specific divine ordinance of the weekly Sabbath rest is something that had to be revealed in Scripture.[36]

Natural Law Principles Outside the Bible?

It is now necessary to consider the controversial question raised at the start of this chapter: Are there natural law principles that are not found in the Bible? Most Protestants are cautious about affirming the existence of moral rules that are not taught clearly in Scripture because they hold to the principle of the sufficiency of Scripture. The *Westminster Confession* states it as follows: "The whole counsel of God concerning all things necessary for His own glory, man's salvation, faith and life, is either expressly set down in Scripture, or by good and necessary consequence may be deduced from Scripture: unto which nothing at any time is to be added, whether by new revelations of the Spirit, or traditions of men" (*WCF* 1.6).

Extrabiblical moral rules might be thought to undermine the sufficiency of Scripture and burden people's consciences. Nevertheless, the Protestant tradition recognizes that there are some principles that are not expressly taught in Scripture but are morally binding. In the very same paragraph as that just quoted, the *Westminster Confession* also states that "there are some circumstances concerning the worship of God, and government of the Church, common to human actions and

36. See also Daniel Cawdry and Herbert Palmer, *Sabbatum Redivivum; or, the Christian Sabbath Vindicated* (London: Thomas Maxey, 1652), 2:18; James Durham, *The Law Unsealed; or, A Practical Exposition of the Ten Commandments* (Glasgow, 1676), 24; William Twisse, *The Christian Sabbath Defended* (London: printed for Thomas Pierrepoint, 1652), 58, 191.

societies, which are to be ordered by the light of nature, and Christian prudence, according to the general rules of the Word, which are always to be observed" (*WCF* 1.6). The "light of nature" referred to in this paragraph is reason—that is, the inbuilt witness to the natural law. The *Confession* recognizes that the light of nature (or natural law) teaches principles that are relevant to church worship and government that must always be observed.

What are these principles? The treatise *The Divine Right of Church-Government*, which was written by various ministers and published around the time the *Westminster Confession* was completed and is often considered to be the Westminster Assembly's defense of Presbyterian church government, gives three examples of principles that are found in the "light of nature" and even states that such principles are of "divine right":

> In the present case of church government, that which is agreeable to the true light of nature must necessarily be confessed to be of *jure divino* [divine right]. Though light of nature is but dim, yet it will lend some help in this particular. For example, light of nature teaches:
>
> > (1) That as every society in the world has a distinct government of its own within itself, without which it could not subsist, so must the church, which is a society, have its own distinct government within itself, without which it cannot subsist, no more than any other society.
> >
> > (2) That in all matters of difference, the lesser number in every society should give way to, and the matters controverted be determined and concluded by the major part; else there would never be an end. And why not so in the Church?
> >
> > (3) That in every ill-administration in inferior societies, the parties grieved should have liberty to appeal from them to

> superior societies, that equity may take place. And why not from inferior to superior church assemblies?[37]

This helps us to see more clearly that the *Westminster Confession* recognizes the existence of principles arising from the light of nature or reason that are not directly taught in Scripture and states that these principles "are always to be observed," in worship and church government. Affirming the existence and applicability of principles that are not expressly taught in Scripture is consistent with the Protestant confessional tradition.

Protestants are rightly cautious about pronouncements on extrascriptural principles. Nevertheless, it is simply not the case that we act and make decisions having regard only to Scripture. The Bible itself draws many conclusions from the world (e.g., Prov. 15:1; 18:17) and commands us to learn from the creation (6:6–8). Isaiah 28 describes the wisdom of the farmer who farms his land with understanding of how the soil functions as instruction from God (v. 26).

This leaves open an intriguing and controversial possibility. If moral principles not found in Scripture can exist, what are they? I suggest that there are three kinds.

Deductions from Natural Law

First, deductions can be made from natural law. These can make explicit the requirements of the natural law in a particular context and lead us to truths that are an outworking of scriptural teaching but not specifically stated in Scripture.

An example is the wrongness of racial discrimination and slavery, which follows from the Golden Rule. We should treat

37. Chris Coldwell, ed., *Jus Divinum Regiminis Ecclesiastici; or, The Divine Right of Church-Government* (Naphtali Press and Reformation Heritage Books, 2020), 62.

others as we would be treated; from this we can conclude that racial discrimination and slavery are wrong. These are not themselves primary precepts of the natural law and are not directly prohibited in Scripture but are specific contexts in which you ought to treat others as you would want to be treated.

George Gillespie considered that it follows from the Golden Rule and human sociability that "we should not offend other men; that we should keep promises; stand to bargains; give to every man his own."[38] In like vein, John Rawls, a twentieth-century non-Christian political philosopher, argued that a capacity for a sense of justice "would appear to be a condition of human sociability."[39]

Thus, principles can be derived by deduction from the precepts of the natural law that go beyond what is directly taught by Scripture, which is similar to the derivation of principles from Scripture "by good and necessary consequence" (*WCF* 1.6).

An Intermediate Category

Second, I suggest that there is an intermediate category between morally neutral and morally binding. That is, there are some principles that form part of the created order but that cannot be expressed as moral rules or laws. Christians sometimes wish to reduce things to black-and-white categories. But reality is not always so tidy. The Bible itself recognizes that it can be good and wise to do something, even though it is not commanded, and that it can be bad and unwise to do something, even though it is not forbidden (e.g., 1 Cor. 10:23).

38. Gillespie, *English-Popish Ceremonies*, 362.
39. John Rawls, *A Theory of Justice*, rev. ed. (Belknap Press, 1999), 433.

Recall that natural law is the principle that there is a created order, and that this order cannot be exhausted by rules. This suggests that there is more to God's moral order than the precepts of the moral law that are summarized in the Decalogue. Francisco Suárez considered that some things are not intrinsically evil but are unbecoming and involve a danger of moral harm, such as the sale of judicial offices or bestowing a spiritual favor consequent upon the offering of a temporal gift.[40] These things are not wrong of themselves but are certainly unadvisable.

As I have already noted, Genesis 2:18, 23–24 states that "it is not good that the man should be alone," which sets out a principle of sociability and companionship, suggesting that it is good for people to marry. That is, it is a good thing, desirable, and consistent with our natural inclinations that we should seek marriage. However, this cannot be reduced to a rule or command. Not all people will marry, there is no imperative for every person to marry, and it is not a sin to remain unmarried (see generally 1 Cor. 7).

In Genesis 1, God told humans to "be fruitful and multiply and fill the earth and subdue it" (v. 28). Thus, it is part of the natural order that people should marry and have children. This sets out a general principle of fruitfulness, and so people and especially Christians should be open to marrying and having children. However, this cannot be neatly translated into specific rules as to (for example) how many children we ought to have.

Similar comments could be made about the respective natures of men and women. Other examples could be given. It is good to develop a skill or craft, to read widely and gain knowledge, to exercise regularly, to take walks in nature, to get into a good

40. Suárez, "A Treatise on Laws," 562.

routine, to sleep well, to look at good art, to shop local, and to grow your own vegetables, but it is not morally obligatory to do all these things. And there are things that are bad or unwise but not of themselves sinful, such as regularly eating ultra-processed foods, having an untidy house, being disorganized, not dressing appropriately for the weather, and spending too much time gaming or on social media.

The nature of reality as created by God suggests that there may be things that form part of the created order that are good or wise but that cannot be stated in terms of rules or precepts.[41] Natural law helps to expand our ethical vocabulary beyond simplistic black-and-white categories.

Examples of Extrabiblical Precepts

Third, I venture to suggest that there *are* some precepts that are not found in the Bible, but ought to be considered morally binding. Jesus condemned those who treat the commandments of men as if they are as authoritative as Scripture (Matt. 15:9; Mark 7:7), and so we ought to be cautious about declaring extrabiblical moral truths. Nevertheless, it seems necessary to recognize some moral truths not contained in Scripture, not as an attempt to invent autonomous moral principles, but rather as a recognition of what is self-evident in or can be deduced from the moral order inscribed by God in creation. Examples of extrabiblical precepts include the following.

Slavery. Notoriously, Scripture never unambiguously forbids slavery.[42] And yet few today would disagree with the prop-

41. O. M. T. O'Donovan, "Towards an Interpretation of Biblical Ethics," *Tyndale Bulletin* 27 (1976): 54–55.

42. Some parts of Scripture appear to condone slavery: Exod. 21:2–11; Lev. 25:44–46; Deut. 20:10–15; 21:10–14; Eph. 6:5–7; Col. 3:22–24.

osition that slavery is morally wrong.[43] The inherent dignity of humans as made in the image of God demands the view that slavery is morally wrong. Subject to exceptions such as punishment for crime, the involuntary deprivation of liberty is wrong. Thus, as a general principle, slavery is evil and contrary to the natural law, even though it is not specifically condemned in Scripture. William Blackstone argues that slavery—that is, where "an absolute and unlimited power" is given to a master over a slave—is "repugnant to reason, and the principles of natural law."[44]

Discrimination. Similarly, although discrimination on ethnic or racial grounds is not clearly prohibited by the Bible, and not all Christians have considered it to be so, it is a clear (and, to modern thinkers, obvious) deduction from natural law principles, especially the dignity of all humans made in God's image and the Golden Rule, that such discrimination is wrong.

Self-defense. Scripture does not clearly affirm a right to self-defense. Nevertheless, thinkers in the Christian tradition have often held that there is a right based on natural law to use proportionate force to defend oneself. For example, George Gillespie wrote that the first precept of the law of nature is "that man seek his own conservation, and avoid his own destruction. Whereupon this conclusion necessarily follows, that he may repel violence with violence."[45]

43. See, e.g., article 8 of the *International Covenant on Civil and Political Rights*, which states that "no one shall be held in slavery; slavery and the slave-trade in all their forms shall be prohibited."

44. Sir William Blackstone, *Commentaries on the Laws of England*, 9th ed. (Oxford University Press, 2016 [1783]), 1:272. See also John Fortescue, *On the Laws and Governance of England*, ed. Shelley Lockwood (Cambridge University Press, 1997), 61.

45. Gillespie, *English-Popish Ceremonies*, 361. See also Aquinas, *ST* II-II, 64.7.

Suicide and euthanasia. If life is a basic and noninstrumental moral good, then suicide and euthanasia are contrary to the natural law.[46]

Cannibalism. Cannibalism is another example of something that is not clearly prohibited by Scripture but which the Christian tradition has almost universally recognized to be wrong.[47] Francisco de Vitoria argued that there is no precept against cannibalism in divine law but that "all nations have always held it to be abominable" and historians and poets describe it "as an unspeakable and inhuman act of savagery,"[48] which is likely the reason why there is no express biblical command not to eat human flesh.

Right to burial. Francisco de Vitoria considered that "burial is clearly a right in natural law."[49] Consider these words from a decision of the Federal Court of Australia: "The story of the Western Australian Aboriginal leader, Yagan, and his death at the hands of two young settlers in 1833 is a tale of colonial tragedy. It has sadly familiar overtones of mutual incomprehension, fear, prejudice, and retribution. The sequel to his death, the severing and smoking of his head and its removal to England for display in a museum, demonstrated a contempt for his humanity which is striking even at this historical remove."[50] Natural law principles lead to the conclusion that everyone has a right to proper burial.

War. Jacques Maritain argues that "do not harm your fellow men" is a precept of the natural law, and also that "treat prisoners

46. Walker, *Faithful Reason*, 266–67.

47. The Bible in various places recognizes that cannibalism is a horrific thing to resort to: e.g., Deut. 28:53–57; 2 Kings 6:28–29; Jer. 19:9; Lam. 4:10.

48. Francisco de Vitoria, "On Dietary Laws, or Self-Restraint," in *Political Writings*, ed. Anthony Pagden (Cambridge University Press, 1991), 207–9.

49. de Vitoria, "On Dietary Laws," 210.

50. Bropho v. Human Rights and Equal Opportunity Commission (2004), 135 FCR 105, 107 [1] (French J).

of war humanely" is a logically derivable precept from first principles of the natural law.[51]

Torture. It is morally wrong to extract a confession or information through torture.[52]

Polygamy. Scripture does not unambiguously forbid polygamy, although it does describe its negative consequences.[53] Polygamy is best seen as wrong because it is contrary to the natural order of creation.[54] Polygamy contradicts the design of mutual and exclusive union between a man and woman, damages spousal intimacy, causes domestic strife, encourages selfishness, and weakens the bond between a father and his children.[55] Hemmingsen declared that "whoever has more wives than one at the same time violates the law of nature."[56]

Contracts. Natural law thinkers have argued that consent is necessary in order for a valid contract to come into existence, and that fraud or a lack of consent invalidates the contract.[57] It seems self-evident that a person cannot be considered to have agreed to enter into a contract unless he has consented to do so, and so this is best seen as a principle of the natural law.

Inheritance. Niels Hemmingsen described the inheritance by children of their parents' property as part of the instinct of nature implanted by the Creator and thus part of the natural law.[58]

51. Jacques Maritain, *Natural Law: Reflections on Theory and Practice*, ed. William Sweet (St. Augustine's Press, 2001), 50, 52.

52. See Fortescue, *On the Laws and Governance of England*, 32–33; Lactantius, *The Divine Institutes, Books I–VII*, trans. Mary Francis McDonald (Catholic University of America Press, 1964), 418.

53. E.g., Gen. 29–30.

54. Not all thinkers have thought it to be absolutely inconsistent with the natural law. Aquinas concluded that "plurality of wives is in a way against the law of nature, and in a way not against it": Aquinas, *ST*, Suppl. 65.2.

55. See https://www.undergroundthomist.org/polygamy.

56. Hemmingsen, *On the Law of Nature*, 10, 97.

57. Suárez, "A Treatise on Laws," 289.

58. Hemmingsen, *On the Law of Nature*, 125.

No one shall be judge in his own cause. The legal maxim *nemo judex in causa sua* stipulates that no person ought to judge a matter in which they have a personal interest. Not all have accepted that this is part of the natural law;[59] nevertheless, it seems clear that a person who has a stake in the outcome of a decision will be unable to decide impartially. The principle follows from the need for justice to be impartial, and so it ought to be regarded as a binding principle (or conclusion) of the natural law.[60]

In claiming that we ought to recognize these principles, I follow Matthew Barrett's caution that they are subject to the authority of Scripture, which alone is infallible.[61] But failing to recognize these as moral truths would mean accepting that slavery, discrimination, polygamy, and cannibalism are morally acceptable.

The Content of Natural Law: A Summary

Below I have attempted to summarize the principles of the natural law laid out in this chapter by compiling a more detailed list of the content of natural law.[62] I do not presume that this list is perfect, but I have included it because surprisingly few books on natural law attempt an explanation of its content.

59. Grotius considered that it was a principle of positive, not natural law: Hugo Grotius, *A Defence of the Catholic Faith Concerning the Satisfaction of Christ*, trans. Frank Hugh Foster (Warren F. Draper, 1889), 56.

60. Francisco Suárez, "A Work on the Three Theological Virtues: Faith, Hope and Charity," in *Selections from Three Works*, ed. Thomas Pink, trans. Gwladys L. Williams et al. (Liberty Fund, 2015), 933.

61. Barrett, *God's Word Alone*, 344.

62. My list includes additional primary precepts, as well as principles derived from those precepts, and so is more detailed than the five primary precepts listed by Aquinas, which, as noted above, were not intended to be exhaustive. The list has been drawn from a wide range of sources including Aquinas, *ST* I-II, 94.2; Walker, *Faithful Reason*, 200–201; Suárez, "A Treatise on Laws"; William of Ockham, *A Short Discourse on Tyrannical Government*, ed. Arthur Stephen McGrade, trans. John Kilcullen (Cambridge University Press, 1992); de Vitoria, *Political Writings*.

The fundamental and primary precept of the natural law is to do good and avoid evil (*ST* I-II, 94.2). The good that is to be done and the evil to be avoided includes the following:

The Knowledge and Worship of God

- There is a God, who is to be worshiped and obeyed.
- People should seek to know God and the manner of his worship.
- A due proportion of time should be set apart for the worship of God.

Human Life

- Human life should be preserved.
- All people are equal in dignity.
- Do not kill the innocent or harm your fellow humans.
- Abortion, cannibalism, torture, suicide, and euthanasia are prohibited.
- Health, rest, and the body are goods; one must live temperately.
- A person may use proportionate force in self-defense.
- All people have the right to a proper burial.

Marriage, Procreation, and Family

- Humans have been created male and female.
- Sex is for marriage. Sins such as adultery, incest, and polygamy are prohibited.
- The conception and bearing of children through the union of male and female in marriage is a good that should be pursued.
- Parents have a duty to care for, nurture, and educate their children.

Humans as Rational and Social Beings

- The Golden Rule: Do to others as you would have them do to you.
- Humans should seek knowledge of the truth. Lying is prohibited.
- Friendship and sociability are goods to be pursued.
- Do not unreasonably give offense to those among whom one has to live.
- Be thankful for gifts.
- Agreements should be performed, vows and promises adhered to.
- Play and aesthetic appreciation (beauty) are goods to be sought.
- Vocation, work, and skillfulness are goods to be sought.
- Slavery and discrimination on racial grounds are prohibited.

Justice and Order

- Humans are social and political by nature; human societies should establish civil government and law.
- There should be no civil or criminal liability without fault.
- Punishment should be proportionate to the offense.
- Give honor and respect to those to whom it is due, including parents, pastors, and rulers.
- Private vengeance is prohibited.
- Justice should be done and injustice avoided. Justice renders to everyone their due.
- All people are equal before the law.

- No one should be penalized without being heard, and no one should be judge in their own cause.
- There should be a right of appeal in cases of maladministration.
- The majority should decide disputed matters.

Property

- Theft and excessive interest are wrong.
- One should give generously out of one's superfluous possessions.
- Borrowed property must be returned.
- Children inherit their parents' property.

Other principles have been suggested by various writers, for example, the hospitable treatment of strangers and travelers,[63] the humane treatment of prisoners of war,[64] a common right of access to roads,[65] the right of rulers to raise and collect taxes,[66] and the provision of compensation for compulsory acquisition of property.[67]

Conclusion

This chapter has focused on the content of the natural law. I have argued in this chapter that, while the natural law and the Decalogue appear very different at face value, they are complementary means of reflecting on the same truth. As noted in chapter 1, the basic principle of natural law is that there is a

63. Francisco de Vitoria, "On the American Indians," in *Political Writings*, ed. Anthony Pagden (Cambridge University Press, 1991), 278.
64. Maritain, *Natural Law*, 50.
65. Ptolemy of Lucca, *On the Government of Rulers*, 130.
66. Ptolemy of Lucca, *On the Government of Rulers*, 179.
67. Finnis, *Natural Law and Natural Rights*, 288.

moral order in creation. This order finds expression in moral rules and laws, which are summarized in the Decalogue. The Decalogue is an authoritative statement of the moral law, but it does not exhaust the moral order.

Reflecting on natural law in the light of Scripture, and reflecting on Scripture in the light of natural law, leads to a richer understanding of both and avoids the twin problems of speculation and arbitrariness. That is, moral prescriptions imposed without reference to Scripture can be overconfident and inaccurate. Anchoring the moral law within the truths of Scripture ensures we have a correct understanding of the moral order. On the other hand, imposing moral prescriptions without any sense of the moral order within which those prescriptions are given can result in a narrow and arbitrary catalog of laws without any apparent rationale.

4

The Moral Order

In chapter 1, I noted that two key points underlie the doctrine of natural law: first, an objective, ordered reality, and second, the knowability of that reality through reason and conscience. Chapters 4 and 5 expand on these issues. This chapter explores the moral order, and chapter 5 discusses the knowability of natural law. How does natural law relate to human nature, especially given that human nature is corrupted by sin? How can we reconcile the "law" and the "natural" in natural law?

The term *natural law* reflects the fact that there is a moral order built into the nature of things—namely, the objective reality of the creation as ordered and purposeful. As eloquently put by Oliver O'Donovan: "The order of things that God has made is *there*. It is objective, and mankind has a place within it. Christian ethics, therefore, has an objective reference because it is concerned with man's life in accordance with this order. The summons to live in it is addressed to all mankind, because the good news that we *may* live in it is addressed to all mankind. Thus Christian moral judgments in principle address every man. . . . They are founded on reality as God has given it."[1]

The primary meaning of natural law is that of an ordered reality. As stated in chapter 1, it is not necessary to be wedded to the term *natural law*; other terms such as *creation ethics* or *moral order* express a similar concept.[2] However, the term *natural law* is well entrenched in Christian thought.

Natural law, then, is the idea of a moral order embedded in creation. Hugo Grotius expressed this point when he said that "the Maxims of the Law of Nature are not merely arbitrary Rules, but are founded on the Nature of Things; on the very Constitution of Man, from which certain Relations result, between such and such Actions, and the State of a reasonable and sociable Creature."[3]

There has been a great deal of debate throughout history about the best way to explain the nature of the created and moral order. Although much more could be said, we can describe the nature of this moral order in the following way.

First, the moral order was created by God. The world is not simply a random collection of atoms but is a "wisely ordered creation" that reflects the goodness and wisdom of its Creator: "The reality we inhabit is a divinely created order, a harmonious cosmos."[4] God made the world "very good" (Gen. 1:31; 1 Cor. 14:33). Christ is central to the creation, for by him all things

1. Oliver O'Donovan, *Resurrection and Moral Order: An Outline for Evangelical Ethics*, 2nd ed. (Eerdmans, 1994), 17.

2. Oliver Barclay argues that "creation ethics" is preferable to natural law: "The Nature of Christian Morality," in *Law, Morality and the Bible: A Symposium*, ed. Bruce Kaye and Gordon Wenham (InterVarsity Press, 1978).

3. Hugo Grotius, *The Rights of War and Peace*, ed. Richard Tuck (Liberty Fund, 2005 [1625]), 1:89n1.

4. Armin Wenz, "Natural Law and the Orders of Creation," in *Natural Law: A Lutheran Reappraisal*, ed. Robert C. Baker (Concordia Publishing House, 2011), 88; Abigail Favale, *The Genesis of Gender: A Christian Theory* (Ignatius Press, 2022), 36.

were created and in him everything holds together (Col. 1:16–17; John 1:3). Natural law does not posit that an autonomous realm exists but that God has left his stamp on his creation.

One implication of this is that the moral order is objectively meaningful. The concept of "order" reflects that there is a predictability and regularity to the world, which is a necessary precondition for moral behavior: Virtues such as thrift, generosity, honesty, and prudence could not exist in a world characterized by total chaos or randomness.[5]

Of course, humans have power to mold aspects of the creation in various ways, but the fundamental contours of reality are determined by God. It is something humans respond to rather than create. In direct contradiction of the modern gender paradigm, there is intrinsic meaning in the world, reality exists prior to our naming it, and our language is meaningful when it corresponds to that reality.[6] This could be described as metaphysical realism—namely, the principle that "things in this world (including human beings) have objectively meaningful natures, and that human nature entails certain obligations and rights, the knowledge of which is accessible to the human mind."[7]

A second implication is that the creation reveals God's character.[8] Scripture in many places draws on the imagery of creation to depict and describe who God is: John Frame wrote that "everything in creation bears some analogy to God. . . . The universe and everything in it symbolizes God."[9] This tells

5. See e.g., Gen. 8:20–22; David S. Oderberg, "The Metaphysical Foundations of Natural Law," in *Natural Moral Law in Contemporary Society*, ed. Holger Zaborowski (Catholic University of America Press, 2010), 47–58.

6. Favale, *Genesis of Gender*, 30–31, 43.

7. VanDrunen, *Divine Covenants and Moral Order*, 23.

8. Several scriptural passages speak of creation declaring the glory of God and his handiwork: e.g., Ps. 19:1–4; Rom. 1:19–20.

9. John M. Frame, *The Doctrine of the Knowledge of God* (P&R, 1987), 230.

us about God's character, and also tells us something about the nature of creation—namely, that it is revelatory and symbolic: "Everything the divine persons created says something about the divine glory."[10]

Thinkers in the Christian tradition have often defined the moral order in teleological terms—that is, that all things are inherently directed to an end or purpose. For many thinkers, a thing's essence or identity is connected with its purpose.[11] Aristotle famously wrote that "every art and every inquiry, and similarly every action and choice, is thought to aim at some good; and for this reason the good has rightly been declared to be that at which all things aim."[12] What is good for a thing is "that end towards which each thing directs itself according to its nature."[13] According to such an approach, the concept of a defined nature presupposes that "there exists an ideal form and function of what something ought to be," defined by reference to its purpose and design.[14] Creation is teleologically ordered to its Creator, as well as horizontally ordered among its parts.[15]

Theologians have also discerned relationality in the creation, reflecting that God himself is both one and three. Peter Leithart has argued that the trinitarian pattern of mutual indwelling and relation to other things is present in every aspect of creation.[16] Like the Trinity, "the world, created according to the

10. McDermott, *Everyday Glory*, 50.

11. E.g., Favale, *Genesis of Gender*, 225; Jensen, *Knowing the Natural Law*, 228.

12. Aristotle, *The Nicomachean Ethics*, trans. David Ross (Oxford University Press, 2009), 1.1 [1094a].

13. David Haines and Andrew Fulford, *Natural Law: A Brief Introduction and Biblical Defense* (Davenant Trust, 2017), 35.

14. Walker, *Faithful Reason*, 147–49, 128–29.

15. O'Donovan, *Resurrection and Moral Order*, ch. 2.

16. Peter Leithart, *Traces of the Trinity: Signs of God in Creation and Human Experience* (Brazos Press, 2015).

divine model, is a web of relationships," and so "everything is interconnected."[17]

Natural Law and Human Nature

How does this relate to natural law? One important aspect of the moral order is human nature, which plays a key part in natural law. Natural law argues that some things are good for humans and some things are not. Natural law theorists often argue that the content of natural law is that which is good, and what is good is defined by human nature. Christian ethics are not a set of arbitrary rules but relate to the way we have been made: "To act in accordance with our nature means to act consistently with the way we are designed to function."[18] God's commands fit our nature.[19]

It is important to appreciate that the natural law concept of "human nature" does not mean the way we are—that is, the way humans habitually act. Instead, "human nature" is a normative concept: It is the way we have been made to function. Natural law is a moral order that directs people "to ways of life that promote and attain the purposes for which God designed them."[20] Natural law seeks to define human nature and those things that are good for humans.[21]

The moral law is sometimes thought of as a series of rules imposed from without: "do not murder," "do not commit

17. Pope Francis, *Laudato Si'* (May 24, 2015), [240]. See also Aquinas, *ST* I, 45.7.

18. Kody W. Cooper and Justin Buckley Dyer, *The Classical and Christian Origins of American Politics: Political Theology, Natural Law, and the American Founding* (Cambridge University Press, 2022), 9; Barclay, "The Nature of Christian Morality."

19. John E. Hare, *God's Call: Moral Realism, God's Commands, and Human Autonomy* (Eerdmans, 2001), 77.

20. David VanDrunen, *Politics After Christendom: Political Theology in a Fractured World* (Zondervan, 2020), 135.

21. Grotius, *The Rights of War and Peace*, 1:152–3.

adultery," and so on. But it can also be seen as inherent to human nature. That is, humans have an inbuilt inclination to do the things commanded by the natural law—for instance, we have a natural desire for sexual union, and we naturally recoil at evils such as murder.

Therefore, a natural law approach to ethics holds "that the basic goods are grounded in human nature."[22] What is good according to natural law is defined by the nature of a thing, according to the attributes given to it by God, the Creator.[23] Natural law posits the existence of an objective moral order "that determines the natural ends, goods, or goals of our existence."[24] Owen Anderson expresses this point well: "God, as creator of human nature, is the determiner of good and evil for humans. So the moral law commanded by God is given not apart from human nature as an imposition . . . but in unison with God creating human nature."[25] The existence of a divinely given moral order means that it is not just wrong to sin, a breach of a moral rule, but it is foolish, irrational, and contrary to our nature.[26]

What, then, is human nature? Arguably the most fundamental point is that human nature is given by God.[27] This is in contrast to the understanding of human nature infamously articulated in 1992 by Justice Anthony Kennedy of the United States Supreme Court: "At the heart of liberty is the right to define one's own concept of existence, of meaning, of the

22. Crowe, *Natural Law and the Nature of Law*, 30, 64; Finnis, *Natural Law and Natural Rights*, 34, 72–73, 81, 380, 403.

23. Suárez, "A Treatise on Laws," 232–34; Hemmingsen, *On the Law of Nature*, 65–66, 71.

24. Walker, *Faithful Reason*, 49.

25. Anderson, *The Natural Moral Law*, 8.

26. The Bible speaks of the foolishness and stupidity of, for example, idolatry and denying God: e.g., Ps. 14:1; Rom. 1:21–23.

27. Junius, *Mosaic Polity*, 65.

universe, and of the mystery of human life."[28] The modern gender paradigm also holds that there is no inherent meaning in the body or sexuality, but that meaning is socially constructed by humans. Against this, a natural law perspective affirms that human nature is innate and given rather than constructed.[29] A natural law account of human nature is universalist; that is, "although human practices and goods can and do differ between social contexts, they have common elements attributable to facts about human nature."[30]

Central to the biblical account of human nature is that humans are made in the image of God (Gen. 1:27). There is a consensus today that this image refers to "humanity's office and role as God's earthly delegates," rather than, say, any one particular characteristic such as rationality.[31] That is, the image of God is reflected primarily in the concept of rule, rather than a set of capacities: Humans have been given the task of governing creation under God's ultimate lordship. Of course, in order to exercise that rule, humans need to have the capacity to do so, and so possess attributes such as rationality and sociability.[32] Humans have a unique place within God's world: "You have made him a little lower than the heavenly beings and crowned him with glory and honor. You have given him dominion over the works of your hands; you have put all things under his feet" (Ps. 8:5–6).

Scripture teaches that humans have been made for worship and communion with God (Acts 17:27) and have been given the capacity for reason and rationality (e.g., Prov. 2:2–6; Isa.

28. Planned Parenthood v. Casey, 505 U.S. 833, 851 (1992).

29. Favale, *Genesis of Gender*, 142, 144.

30. Crowe, *Natural Law and the Nature of Law*, 37.

31. Middleton, *The Liberating Image*, 60.

32. Matthew Levering, *Engaging the Doctrine of Creation: Cosmos, Creatures, and the Wise and Good Creator* (Baker Academic, 2017), 145, 191.

1:10; Rom. 12:2). It also teaches that humans are inherently relational and social (Gen. 2:18; Prov. 18:1), with an innate desire for marriage and sexual union (Gen. 2:23–24) and have been made to exercise rule over the creation (Gen. 1:27–28). Further, humans were not created as isolated individuals but exist within the structures of family, church, and state, and fulfill roles within those structures as husband, wife, father, mother, son, daughter, pastor, elder, and magistrate.[33]

God made humans as embodied creatures, as an "integrated unity of body and soul."[34] When he pronounced all creation "very good" (Gen. 1:31), this included the human body, which shares in the dignity of God's image.[35] The body, therefore, is something good that reveals who we are, and not something to be transcended. Similarly, sexual difference, grounded in the body, is constitutive of who we are and "an integral part of the created order, which is *good*."[36]

Writers and thinkers in the natural law tradition have often understood human nature teleologically—that is, by reference to the end or purpose of humans' capacities. On this account, the natural law is the attainment of those purposes for which humans are made; as Aquinas wrote, "It is good for everything that it obtain its end: and its evil is that it turn from its end."[37] The opening question of the *Westminster Shorter Catechism* reflects a teleological view, stating that "man's chief end is to glorify God, and to enjoy him forever."[38]

33. Carl E. Braaten, "A Lutheran Affirmation of the Natural Law," in *Natural Law: A Lutheran Reappraisal*, ed. Robert C. Baker (Concordia Publishing House, 2011), 9.

34. Favale, *Genesis of Gender*, 135.

35. *Catechism of the Catholic Church*, 93 [364].

36. Favale, *Genesis of Gender*, 40.

37. Thomas Aquinas, *Summa Contra Gentiles*, trans. Fathers of the English Dominican Province (Aeterna Press, 2014), 510 [III.122]; Aquinas, *ST* I-II, 99.1.

38. See also Junius, *Mosaic Polity*, 52.

As embodied creatures, our good includes bodily well-being, as well as our "intellectual, moral and spiritual well-being."[39] The nature of humans as made in the image of God as rational and social beings suggests that there are a variety of goods that pertain to human nature, such as "life, family, health, integrity, knowledge of the truth, justice, friendship, play, vocation, integrity, skillfulness, aesthetic experience, authenticity, practical reasonableness, and religion."[40]

But is it not true that there is remarkable diversity among human cultures? And if human nature includes our social as well as biological dispositions,[41] then does this diversity not cast doubt on the idea of a universal human nature?

While there is certainly diversity, especially in relation to language and forms of belief, anthropological research supports the existence of a wide range of universals common to human cultures, such as sociability, the existence of social structures and rules governing behavior, etiquette and friendliness, cooperation and reciprocity, family and kinship, the enculturation of norms in children, ethnicity and the formation of collective identity, religion and belief, logic and reason, art, literature, music, language, emotion, and nonverbal communication.[42] And these are uniquely human. John Finnis appears to be correct in his argument that there seems to be a "universality of a few basic values in a vast diversity of realizations."[43]

39. Robert P. George, "Natural Law, God and Human Dignity," in *The Cambridge Companion to Natural Law Jurisprudence*, ed. George Duke and Robert P. George (Cambridge University Press, 2017), 60.

40. Walker, *Faithful Reason*, 76.

41. Crowe, *Natural Law and the Nature of Law*, 32.

42. Christoph Antweiler, *Our Common Denominator: Human Universals Revisited*, trans. Diane Kerns (Berghahn Books, 2016), ch. 4; Donald E. Brown, *Human Universals* (McGraw-Hill, 1991).

43. Finnis, *Natural Law and Natural Rights*, 83–84, listing life, procreation, cooperation, justice, friendship, property, play, authority, and religion.

Human Nature and the State of Sin

Natural law draws a close connection between the moral law and human nature. However, that nature has been radically corrupted by the fall of humankind, which impairs our ability to know the natural law. Has the fall resulted in a fundamental change in human nature, such that assertions of a natural law are now meaningless?

Some have argued that the fall marks such a decisive break that the image of God is almost entirely effaced.[44] Karl Barth, for instance, considered that the image of God has been "totally annihilated" after the fall: "The image of God is not just, as it is said, destroyed apart from a few relics; it is totally annihilated. . . . No matter how it may be with his humanity and personality, man has completely lost the capacity for God."[45] Humans therefore have no inherent power to form a reliable idea of God apart from his revelation in the Word of God.[46] Obtaining real knowledge of the true God through the creation is "a possibility in principle, but not in fact."[47] Some thinkers see this as fatal to the concept of natural law. Helmut Thielicke argues that it is only possible to speak of natural law if we hold that the entry of sin effects only a limited disturbance, a kind of "subtraction from original perfection," and not a radical corruption of the world and the image of God.[48]

44. For discussion of views that argue for continuity, see Ernst Troeltsch, *The Social Teaching of the Christian Churches*, trans. Olive Wyon (University of Chicago Press, 1981), 1:161–62.

45. Karl Barth, *Church Dogmatics*, ed. G. W. Bromiley and T. F. Torrance, trans. G. W. Bromiley, G. T. Thomson, and Harold Knight (T&T Clark, 2010), I.1, 235.

46. Karl Barth, *Church Dogmatics*, trans. G. W. Bromiley (T&T Clark, 1961), I/1, 238–39; III/1, 346–49.

47. Emil Brunner and Karl Barth, *Natural Theology*, trans. Peter Fraenkel (Geoffrey Bles, 1946), 106.

48. Helmut Thielicke, *Theological Ethics*, ed. William H. Lazareth (Eerdmans, 1979), 1:390, 394, 398, 402.

The better view, I suggest, is that the image is corrupted but not lost. After the fall, in several places Scripture repeats the creation mandate (Gen. 9:1) and restates the truth that humans are made in God's image or likeness (Gen. 9:6; James 3:9). The fall has undoubtedly radically affected human reason, but humans retain rational capacity and will; humans, therefore, are corrupted image bearers, but the image of God has not been entirely lost.[49]

Scripture itself teaches that the original moral order has ongoing normative force. In Mark 10:6–9 Jesus appeals to the creation order to conclude that "what therefore God has joined together, let not man separate." The Sabbath command is expressly grounded in the fact that in six days the Lord made heaven and earth and rested on the seventh day (Exod. 20:8–11). That is, the original creation order remains normative, even though the fall has significantly impaired human ability to perceive and act consistently with that order. Adopting the terminology introduced earlier, this suggests that the consequences of sin are primarily epistemological, not ontological. Human nature is not fundamentally different from human nature prior to the fall.

Calvin argued that the original creation order remains an authoritative pattern and the laws of nature have not changed.[50] He wrote that the image of God has been corrupted in "frightful deformity" but "not totally annihilated and destroyed"; some "sparks still gleam" in man's degenerate nature.[51]

As put by Carl Henry, "However serious its consequences and however far-reaching its effects, the fall of man . . . did not

49. VanDrunen, *Divine Covenants and Moral Order*, 97.

50. Simon P. Kennedy, *Reforming the Law of Nature: The Secularisation of Political Thought, 1532–1689* (Edinburgh University Press, 2022), 34–37.

51. Calvin, *Institutes of the Christian Religion*, 1.15.4; 2.2.12.

involve man's total loss of knowledge of God, nor of his rational competence or ethical accountability. Although sullied by the fall, the divine image in man was not totally shattered . . . even after the fall man is marked off from the animal world by facets of the original image, and lives out his creaturely existence within the forms of reason and morality that distinctively structure human experience."[52]

This suggests, then, that there are areas of continuity and discontinuity both in relation to the image of God pre- and post-fall, and also in terms of the natural law. The *Westminster Confession* teaches that the moral law written on the heart of humans at creation binds both Adam "and all his posterity, to personal, entire, exact, and perpetual obedience"; that is, the law given at creation remains binding as a rule of conduct for all people (*WCF* 4.2, 19.1).

Human Inclinations

Natural law is therefore closely connected with human nature. Human inclinations play an important role in natural law theory, being considered to be one of the ways in which human nature is expressed. Thinkers such as Aquinas appear to define natural law by reference to human inclinations, or at least ground natural laws on natural inclinations:[53] Aquinas writes that "all those things to which man has a natural inclination are naturally apprehended by reason as being good, and consequently as things to be pursued, and their opposites as evil, and as objects to be avoided" (*ST* I-II, 94.2). For Aquinas, human inclinations are the means by which humans participate in the eternal law, and so in a sense, inclinations are constitutive of the natural law.

52. Henry, *God, Revelation, and Authority*, 2:136.
53. Budziszewski, *Treatise on Law*, 248, 267.

Obviously enough, humans have sinful as well as good inclinations, and so not all human inclinations or instincts are morally good or part of the natural law.[54] That is, "natural" does not mean "what naturally occurs"; rather, those inclinations that constitute the natural law are those that are consistent with the purpose or design of human nature.[55] A natural inclination is what humans have been made to pursue and what leads to their well-being.[56]

The human inclinations that make up the natural law are not mere appetites or tendencies but those things that we rationally perceive to be right and that are consistent with our nature. James Keenan defines *inclinations* as "those natural tendencies that need to be rightly realized."[57] Similarly, J. Budziszewski defines "natural inclination" as what is necessary for the fulfillment of our rational nature, which may often be different from what we would like to do.[58]

The content of natural law relates to human inclinations: Things that fulfill human inclinations are good, while things that impede those inclinations are wrong. Human inclinations direct us to pursue certain ends or goods that form part of the natural law, such as fellowship with God, sexual union, and reproduction. For many thinkers, human nature is conceived in teleological terms. That is, a thing's nature is "the design imparted to it by the Creator—as a purpose impressed upon it by the divine art, so that it is directed to a determinate end."[59]

54. Zanchi, *On the Law in General*, 18.

55. Walker, *Faithful Reason*, 147–49.

56. Budziszewski, *Treatise on Law*, 267.

57. James F. Keenan, *A History of Catholic Theological Ethics* (Paulist Press, 2022), 157.

58. Budziszewski, *Treatise on Law*, 216, 289, 427.

59. J. Budziszewski, *Companion to the Commentary* (Cambridge University Press, 2014), 97.

What has been said so far in this chapter reflects two important claims made by classical natural law theory: "First, there is a natural moral order to the universe that is teleological in character; that is, all things in the cosmos, including human beings, seek to fulfill their basic and created purposes and functions, and doing so represents what is the 'good' for each thing, including human beings. Second, this teleological order is discernible in fundamental behavioral inclinations or tendencies in things. For human beings, this means our common human inclinations and indications of what is the 'good' for us, and what it is that enhances human flourishing."[60]

Reconciling Law and Order

The moral order, therefore, is closely related to human nature, which finds expression in human inclinations. The moral order inscribed in creation can be seen as the broader view of natural law (i.e., the *natural* in natural law). How does this relate to the narrow view of natural law, which I have described as the moral law (i.e., the *law* in natural law)? How might we reconcile these two views of the natural law?

Moral law and moral order are best seen as two sides of the same coin. Hemmingsen puts it well: Because "it commands and forbids, it is called 'law,' and because it is implanted in nature, it is called 'natural.'"[61] The rules and precepts that

60. Thomas D. Pearson, "Luther's Pragmatic Appropriation of the Natural Law Tradition," in *Natural Law: A Lutheran Reappraisal*, ed. Robert C. Baker (Concordia Publishing House, 2011), 43.

61. Hemmingsen, *On the Law of Nature*, 29. See also Jean Porter, *Nature as Reason: A Thomistic Theory of the Natural Law* (Eerdmans, 2005), 14, quoting Huguccio: "Reason is said to be a law, because it commands . . . it is said to be natural, because reason is one of the natural goods, or because it agrees supremely with nature."

constitute the moral law reflect this created order; they express important aspects of it, but the moral order is broader than a set of rules. Sin is wrong because it is contrary to God's commands; but more than that, it is bad, unwholesome, and contrary to human nature. Sin is "a disturbance or confusion of the divine order."[62]

Consider a few examples. The first commandment is that "you shall have no other gods before me" (Exod. 20:3; Deut. 5:7). This reflects the reality that God has set eternity in the hearts of humans and that we have been made by God for fellowship and communion with him (Eccles. 3:11; Acts 17:27). Our chief end is to glorify God, and to enjoy him forever; and so, as Augustine famously said, our hearts are restless until they find rest in God.[63] Further, the creation itself is ordered to reflect this, given that God's eternal power and divine nature can be clearly perceived in the things that have been made (Rom. 1:20). Failing to worship God leads a person inevitably to worship the creature (1:25). The rule "you shall have no other gods" therefore reflects human nature and the creation itself.

The biblical teaching on sexuality seems to many people to be an arbitrary set of rules. However, it reflects a broader created reality, including the complementary natures of men and women, the blessings of sexual union within marriage, and the reality that a stable lifelong committed relationship provides the best environment for children to be raised in. The seventh commandment, "you shall not commit adultery," is the tip of a much bigger iceberg.

62. Melanchthon, *Chief Theological Topics*, 48.

63. Augustine, *The Confessions of St. Augustine*, trans. E. B. Pusey (Heron Books, 1962), 1; James Packer, "Conscience, Choice and Character," in *Law, Morality and the Bible: A Symposium*, ed. Bruce Kaye and Gordon Wenham (InterVarsity Press, 1978), 181–82.

David VanDrunen gives a helpful illustration of this point, noting that the seventh commandment "is an important universal rule, but there is a lot more to a successful, lifelong marriage relationship and to training children toward responsible adulthood." Love, kindness, commitment, communication, physical affection, trust, and many other things are also essential. Why not have a longer list of rules that outline what is necessary for a successful lifelong marriage? Given the uniqueness and diversity of human existence, it is not possible to formulate a prescriptive set of rules for family life that would apply equally well to all people.[64]

We could make similar comments about each of the Ten Commandments. Each commandment reflects a broader moral order and encapsulates something of that order. "Creation itself demands life in accordance with the will of the Creator, and the Torah, or at least the principles which it embodies, is the most perfect expression of law that is in accordance with creation rightly understood."[65]

The Vagueness of the Created Order

I have argued that a core principle of natural law is the existence of a moral order. One interesting feature of this is that there is a level of vagueness or uncertainty to natural law. The moral law, as expressed in the precepts of the Decalogue, is not vague. But the moral order is broader than moral rules or laws. And there is a level of vagueness relating to the created order. Or to put the point more precisely, it is not always possible to define and describe the moral order in watertight propositions.

Consider the differences between the sexes. There is a clear difference between men and women, evident in such things as

64. VanDrunen, *Politics After Christendom*, 135–36.
65. Bockmuehl, "Natural Law in Second Temple Judaism," 28.

different tendencies and biological characteristics.[66] But these differences are a matter of degree, and it is difficult to give a definition that captures all those differences and yet is inclusive enough to cover all people. The Bible does not give us a *definition* of "man" and "woman" but rather presents the gendered reality that God made humanity male and female.

Another example is that Genesis 1 states that "God created man in his own image" (v. 27). There has been enormous controversy throughout the history of the church as to what the image of God consists of. Some argue that it relates to human relationality, others to rational capacities or the ability to perceive right and wrong, and others see it as related primarily to the exercise of rule. The Bible clearly states that humans are made in God's image but does not precisely define the content of the image.[67]

Uncertainty or vagueness seems to be an inherent feature of the world. At what moment does a child become an adult? What temperature is hot? When does red shade into orange? What speed is unsafe? How many grains of sand make a heap? We sharply distinguish between big and small, old and young, sane and insane, drunk and sober, democracy and dictatorship, but it is not in fact possible to draw a sharp line demarcating these categories.[68] An English judge expressed this well: "Nothing is more common in life than to be unable to draw the line between two things. Who can draw the line between plants and animals? And yet, who has any difficulty in saying that an oak tree is a plant and not an animal?"[69]

66. McDermott, *Everyday Glory*, 135–37.

67. Henry, *God, Revelation, and Authority*, 2:125.

68. Glanville L. Williams, "Language and the Law," part 2, *Law Quarterly Review* 61 (1945): 179, 182.

69. Attorney-General v. Brighton and Hove Co-Operative Supply Association [1900] 1 Ch 276, 282 (Lindley MR).

Given this, it is perhaps not surprising that there is a level of vagueness or inexactitude to the natural law.[70] This can be seen in the following ways. The first is the definition and articulation of its precepts. According to Aquinas, the first precept of the natural law is that "whatever is a means of preserving human life belongs to the natural law, and whatever impedes it is contrary to it" (*ST* I-II, 94.2). While the basic point is intuitively obvious, translating this into a specific course of action will evidently require careful thought. And it is not clear that the precept could be expressed with more precision.

Second, I argued in the previous chapter that there is an intermediate category between morally binding and morally neutral. It is often difficult to translate things that fall in this intermediate category into specific rules or precepts. For example, children are a blessing, and Christians ought to be open to marrying and having children, but when to have children, and how many to have, is a matter of wisdom rather than prescription.

As a result, many principles of the natural law are general precepts whose application depends on the circumstances. An example given by Suárez is "the natural precept on the keeping of secrets." We should generally keep secrets entrusted to us, but if a greater necessity arises such as the protection of life, the precept may be violated.[71] Likewise, Aquinas says we should generally return property that has been entrusted to us, but if that property is intended to be used by an enemy or for violent purposes, then the property should not be restored.[72]

There is biblical support for the idea I am seeking to convey. There are, of course, exceptionless prohibitions such as

70. David S. Oderberg, *Moral Theory: A Non-Consequentialist Approach* (Blackwell Publishers, 2000), 4.

71. Suárez, "A Treatise on Laws," 296–98.

72. Aquinas, *ST* II-II, 57.2; Budziszewski, *Treatise on Law*, 284.

those contained in the Decalogue. But many other teachings and commands require the application of prudential wisdom rather than black-and-white rules. For example, Christians are told to obey our civil rulers (Rom. 13:1, 5; 1 Pet. 2:13), and yet Scripture also commends those who disobey unjust rulers (e.g., Dan. 3; 6; Acts 4:19–20). Proverbs enjoins us to not answer a fool according to his folly lest we become like him and immediately afterward enjoins the precise opposite (26:4–5). Paul's discussion of whether believers should marry concludes with these words: "He who marries his betrothed does well, and he who refrains from marriage will do even better" (1 Cor. 7:38).

Reasoning in a world where distinctions are necessary but cannot be drawn with precision means that many of our actions and decisions are based on practical wisdom or good judgment rather than absolute certainty.[73]

The Natural Law as Non-Absolute Goods

Another important feature of the principles of natural law is that they are not absolute goods to be pursued at all times. There are two exceptions to this. Our duty to worship and obey the one true God is absolute. And as I have noted, precepts of the natural law as expressed in the Ten Commandments, such as "do not murder" and "do not commit adultery," are not subject to exceptions. But there are many aspects of the moral order that are not absolute. Take, for example, the good of play: Obviously enough, this should not be pursued all the time. Someone who pursues knowledge and work but is friendless and ignores his family would rightly be seen as unbalanced and

73. Dorothy Edgington, "The Philosophical Problem of Vagueness," *Legal Theory* 7, no. 4 (2001): 371, 372.

neglectful. Enjoyment of aesthetic experience, friendship, and sociability is for most people likely to be episodic, as are some aspects of the good of "religion," such as corporate worship.

Pursuing something to excess is likely to undermine that very thing: "More of a good thing is not necessarily better."[74] Eating and exercising are ways to promote the goods of life and health, but it does not follow that we should be eating and exercising all the time. There are questions of both time and balance in relation to our pursuit of the goods: "For everything there is a season, and a time for every matter under heaven" (Eccles. 3:1–8). It is also true that the removal of a good thing can be a good thing. God often afflicts his children with ill health or other evils so as to (for example) discipline or sanctify them.

Consequences

Natural law is the principle that God has made the world according to a moral order. If humans violate that order, we are violating the way we were intended to function, so to speak, and that will have consequences. Consequences, therefore, are witnesses to the natural law. This is not consequentialism (the view that the consequences of an action are determinative of its moral rightness). But Scripture teaches clearly that sin has consequences.[75] As Richard Hooker observes, "Good does follow to all things by observing the course of their nature, and on the contrary side evil by not observing it."[76]

The Wisdom Literature of the Old Testament can be seen as an explanation of the order embedded in the world, in which there is a correspondence between the natural world and human

74. Crowe, *Natural Law and the Nature of Law*, 67.
75. E.g., Ps. 7:14–16; Prov. 1:18–19; 5:1–14; 6:27–29.
76. Hooker, *Laws*, 1:69 [1.9.1].

actions, and consequences generally follow from actions.[77] There is of course no automatic correlation, but diligence tends to produce wealth while laziness tends to produce poverty (e.g., Prov. 10:4); "whatever one sows, that will he also reap" (Gal. 6:7).

Those who do not honor the true and living God will end up worshiping and serving the creature rather than the Creator, and their thinking is darkened (Rom. 1:21–25). By contravening the moral law, men receive in themselves "the due penalty for their error" (v. 27). If you regularly tell lies, people stop trusting you. Those who abandon their children have no one to comfort them in old age.[78] Divorce typically leads to lower levels of happiness and to economic pressures, and it seriously impacts children. Promiscuity is strongly linked to depression and carries other risks such as emotional and psychological harm, sexually transmitted disease, sexual violence, and unintended pregnancy.[79] "Every sin against God abates, and continuance in sin extinguishes, our love towards him."[80]

These consequences provide evidence both of the existence of the moral law and its inherent connection with human nature. The moral law is hardwired into creation, and if we violate it, there will be consequences.

Conclusion

This chapter has explored the nature of the moral order, its connection with human nature, and how a broader concept of moral order relates to the narrower preceptive concept of

77. Barton, *Ethics in Ancient Israel*, 97, 115.

78. J. Budziszewski, *What We Can't Not Know: A Guide*, rev. ed. (Ignatius Press, 2011), 104.

79. Justin R. Garcia et al., "Sexual Hookup Culture: A Review," *Review of General Psychology* 16, no. 2 (2012): 161, 168.

80. Hooker, *Laws*, 3:8 [6.3.3].

moral law. It has also discussed how there is a vagueness to the created order, such that it cannot always be expressed in watertight propositions. As such, reasoning with natural law is often a matter of practical wisdom or good judgment.

This raises the question, How might we reason using natural law? I will discuss this in the next chapter.

5

Natural Law Reasoning

Perhaps the most common Protestant objection to natural law is that it fails adequately to take account of human sin. Many Protestants think that natural law (especially as found in Thomist accounts) is too optimistic about the ability of fallen humans to discern the moral law.[1] It is a core element of Protestant (and scriptural) doctrine that "in addition to the ignorance of the mind and a turning-away from God in the heart, there clings in all people a propensity for knowing and doing those things which God's law prohibits."[2] Humans naturally suppress the knowledge of the truth in unrighteousness (Rom. 1:18), and so our thinking about morality is often flawed. Thus, although there is an objective moral order inherent in creation, there is no certainty that humans can interpret it correctly without divine revelation.[3] Carl F. H. Henry sums

1. E.g., Carl F. H. Henry, *Twilight of a Great Civilization: The Drift Toward Neo-Paganism* (Crossway Books, 1988), 33.

2. William Den Boer and Riemer A. Faber, eds., *Synopsis of a Purer Theology*, trans. Riemer A. Faber (Davenant Press, 2023), 1:150.

3. O'Donovan, *Resurrection and Moral Order*, 19.

up the thoughts of many Protestants when he says that natural law "does not take sufficient cognizance of the epistemic impact of sin upon the life of man."[4]

Are these critiques fatal to the concept of natural law or the existence of self-evident moral truths? How can we know the natural law, especially if human reasoning is corrupted by sin? God alone is lord of the conscience, and we ought to be cautious about imposing extrabiblical moral precepts under the guise of natural law. How can we reason with natural law in a manner that avoids binding the conscience?

This chapter discusses how to know the natural law and reason with natural law concepts, introducing key ideas and terminology from the literature. This chapter argues that natural law is known through reason and the conscience and that although our capacity to reason is distorted by sin, it is nevertheless possible to gain a nonsalvific understanding of aspects of the moral law outside of Scripture.

The Nature of the Principles of Natural Law

Let us first consider what sort of principles the precepts of natural law are. Aquinas argued that reason is inherent to the concept of law, including natural law, defining *law* as an "ordinance of reason" (*ST* I-II, 90.4). That is, moral statements are not simply articulations of a person's attitudes or emotions but can be expressed as rational propositions.

Medieval thinkers and thinkers in the Thomist tradition contrast speculative reason and practical reason. Speculative reason is directed to knowledge of things for their own sake, while practical reason is oriented to doing and aims to determine

4. Henry, "Natural Law and a Nihilistic Culture," 54.

what course of action to pursue.[5] Practical reason "is the mind charting what is to be, not merely recording what already is."[6] The precepts of the natural law are often referred to as principles of practical reason because they are oriented to action.

Chapter 3 discussed the content of natural law, explaining that the principles of natural law can be defined in several ways. In natural law theory, the foundational principles of natural law are often referred to as the primary principles of practical reason.

What is the nature of these principles of natural law? Can we prove their existence? Natural law thinkers argue that the principles of natural law are indemonstrable and self-evident (e.g., *ST* I-II, 94.2). It is not possible to reach or conclude these principles from more foundational truths; they are the foundational principles of morality. That is, they are not conclusions that can be proven but are premises that people reason from. They are principles that are inherently true by virtue of our created nature and that humans recognize as self-evident. As self-evident truths, the precepts of the natural law "are known through themselves, without the need of syllogism" and cannot be concluded from prior demonstration.[7]

Characterizing the truths of the natural law as indemonstrable or self-evident means that when people are taught the moral principles contained in the Ten Commandments, they know instinctively that they are right.[8] "The important thing

5. Lisska, *Aquinas's Theory of Natural Law*, 3; Michael Bertram Crowe, *The Changing Profile of the Natural Law* (Nijhoff, 1977), 169. See also Jensen, *Knowing the Natural Law*, 8–9.

6. Germain G. Grisez, "The First Principle of Practical Reason: A Commentary on the *Summa Theologiae*, 1–2, Question 94, Article 2," *Natural Law Forum* 10 (1965): 175.

7. Jensen, *Knowing the Natural Law*, 4, 28; Hemmingsen, *On the Law of Nature*, 63.

8. McDermott, *Everyday Glory*, 93.

about a self-evident proposition is that people (with the relevant experience, and understanding of terms) assent to it without needing the proof of argument."[9]

The principles of the natural law are noninstrumental: They are not means to an end. They are normative in and of themselves, and so pursuing any of the goods for its own sake "is normally intelligible without further explanation."[10] Another way to put this is that no further reason is needed to explain why a person would pursue a good. For example, take the good of knowledge: Why ought we to pursue the acquisition of knowledge? Simply because knowledge is a good thing. "The principle that truth is worth pursuing, knowledge is worth having, is thus an underived principle. Neither its intelligibility nor its force rests on any further principle."[11]

In our day, many argue that only those things that can be proven scientifically or experienced by the senses should be accepted as valid truths. According to that standard, it would be irrational to believe in indemonstrable moral truths. And it is true that it is not possible to prove logically or scientifically that, for example, it is wrong to abuse children. That does not mean that the natural law is irrational; rather, the principles of practical reason are rationality itself.[12] It would be contrary to the nature of reality (and so irrational) to deny them.[13] Not everything that is true can be proven empirically, such as the proposition that all truth should be demonstrated scientifically.

For example, consider these statements: "It is wrong to kill the innocent," "It is wrong to abuse children," and "All people

9. Finnis, *Natural Law and Natural Rights*, 31.
10. Crowe, *Natural Law and the Nature of Law*, 35.
11. Finnis, *Natural Law and Natural Rights*, 69.
12. C. S. Lewis, *The Abolition of Man* (Geoffrey Bles, 1943), 25.
13. Finnis, *Natural Law and Natural Rights*, 105.

have equal dignity." These are truths that rational people recognize as being true. No sane person would deny that it is wrong to sexually abuse a child. They are not principles that are susceptible of proof: It is impossible to prove logically or scientifically that people have equal dignity or that we should not kill the innocent.

In order to engage in any reasoning, it is necessary to grant the truth of some foundational premises.[14] The scientific method itself presupposes the validity of other principles and norms of rationality that are "undemonstrated, indemonstrable, but self-evident," such as the principles of logic, the ability to study and understand the world through experimentation and observation, and the orderliness, consistency, and predictability of the universe.[15] In any chain of logic or reasoning there has to be a starting point, and in the case of moral reasoning, the principles of natural law or practical reason provide that starting point.

This understanding of the principles of natural law is consistent with Scripture, which (as noted in chapter 2) presupposes the existence of "self-evident standards of morality" and a universal knowledge of moral norms.[16]

The principles of natural law are the foundational principles that provide the essential basis for any system of values. Denying this is likely to mean that there is no possibility of moral judgment. As C. S. Lewis argues, "If nothing is obligatory for its own sake, nothing is obligatory at all."[17] This is because it is not possible to reason to moral obligation from purely factual premises.

14. Jensen, *Knowing the Natural Law*, 27–28.

15. Finnis, *Natural Law and Natural Rights*, 32, 68–70.

16. Bockmuehl, "Natural Law in Second Temple Judaism," 21; Burnside, *God, Justice, and Society*, 76–77; Barton, *Ethics in Ancient Israel*, 101–2.

17. Lewis, *Abolition of Man*, 31; Walker, *Faithful Reason*, 140.

Natural law is the principle of a moral order built into reality. It would be difficult to prove the existence of that order; it is the way things are.[18]

Ironically, this does not seem to be worlds apart from the presuppositional approach advocated by thinkers such as Cornelius Van Til. Van Til argues that "the only 'proof' of the Christian position is that unless its truth is presupposed there is no possibility of 'proving' anything at all. The actual state of affairs as preached by Christianity is the necessary foundation of 'proof' itself."[19] If Christianity is not true, then nothing can be true.[20] Something similar is true for moral truth: Presupposing the existence of God is the necessary starting point, not only for knowledge but also for ethics and moral truth.

Although the principles of natural law cannot be proven, it is possible to reason with those principles, showing, for example, their consistency with human nature and the consequences of breaching the natural law.[21] Natural law provides an analytical tool to assist in explaining the structure of morality imposed on the universe, and thereby providing a reasoned defense of the moral law.[22] Natural law theorists have held that further precepts can be derived from the foundational and indemonstrable principles.[23]

18. Barclay, "The Nature of Christian Morality," 128. Oliver Barclay has argued that the biblical framework provides the best fit and explanation for reality, even though people are not normally convinced by formal logic of its truth.

19. Cornelius Van Til, "My Credo," in *Jerusalem and Athens: Critical Discussions on the Philosophy and Apologetics of Cornelius Van Til*, ed. E. R. Geehan (P&R Publishing, 1971), 21.

20. Cornelius Van Til, *The Defense of the Faith*, 3rd ed. (P&R Publishing, 1967), 208.

21. See Grotius, *The Rights of War and Peace*, 1:159.

22. Walker, *Faithful Reason*, 72.

23. Junius, *Mosaic Polity*, 46.

Another important feature of the principles of natural law is that they are not mere descriptions of the world or statements of fact but have oughtness built into them. That is, the moral law is prescriptive, not merely descriptive. Of their very nature the principles of the natural law are morally obliging. The moral law is not simply a thesis, but an imperative or claim. The inherent worth of all humans demands that we respect human life.[24]

Aquinas's statement that self-preservation is part of the natural law (*ST* I-II, 94.2) is not an inference drawn from the observed empirical fact that living substances seek the preservation of their own being. Rather, it constitutes a recognition that life is inherently a moral good that *should be* preserved. That is, the principle is not that humans do in fact seek to preserve themselves; it is that human life ought to be preserved.

An instructive counterexample is provided by Jordan Peterson, who argues that dominance hierarchies are a pervasive feature of the natural and human world.[25] Despite their widespread persistence, however, this ought not to be seen as a principle of the natural law. That is, it is not the case that dominance hierarchies are a self-evident good and something that humans ought to pursue.

How We Know the Natural Law

The previous section argued that the principles of natural law are indemonstrable and self-evident principles. How do humans know these principles? This is a controversial question in the natural law literature about which volumes have been written.

24. Thielicke, *Theological Ethics*,1:387.

25. Jordan B. Peterson, *12 Rules for Life: An Antidote to Chaos* (Penguin Press, 2019), ch. 1.

Some caution is warranted given that Scripture does not present a detailed epistemology of how we know the natural law.[26]

Scripture teaches that the work of the moral law is written on the hearts of all people and that our consciences bear witness to the natural law, testifying to the truth of its precepts and condemning us when we contravene its requirements (Rom. 2:14–15). The law of nature "has been imprinted by God upon the minds of men."[27]

Conscience is "the subjective human faculty that perceives and responds to the objective natural law promulgated in the created order."[28] The conscience applies the law of God to our conduct, approving that which is done rightly and condemning transgressions.[29] Scripture speaks of God communicating through the witness of "the things that have been made" (1:20).[30] As noted in chapter 2, Scripture assumes that all people are able to perceive moral truth. However, this does not mean that we are born with a complete and accurate knowledge of the moral law. Rather, humans are built to recognize the truths of the natural law, having the capacity of reason and the faculty of conscience, and these capacities need to be correctly informed and instructed. The principles of natural law are self-evident, but they are not innate, inscribed on the mind at birth.[31] They must be learned through experience, reflection, and education. As with any field of study, the natural law is not deduced from

26. VanDrunen, *Divine Covenants and Moral Order*, 254, 480.

27. Hemmingsen, *On the Law of Nature*, 26.

28. David VanDrunen, "Conscience and Natural Law in Scripture," in *Christianity and the Laws of Conscience: An Introduction*, ed. Jeffrey B. Hammond and Helen M. Alvaré (Cambridge University Press, 2021), 39.

29. Melanchthon, *Chief Theological Topics*, 511; Hemmingsen, *On the Law of Nature*, 165.

30. VanDrunen, *Divine Covenants and Moral Order*, 217.

31. Finnis, *Natural Law and Natural Rights*, 65.

reason operating in a vacuum but learned from authoritative texts and sources.[32]

Knowledge is an achievement and must be earned through reflection and experience.[33] For many people knowledge about the world is something we are taught by others, so education and instruction is a key source of moral truth. Knowledge obtained in all these ways is imperfect, and so it is (or needs to be) confirmed or corrected by Scripture.

Calvin states that "God provided man's soul with a mind, by which to distinguish good from evil, right from wrong; and, with the light of reason as guide, to distinguish what should be followed from what should be avoided."[34] Thus, knowledge of the natural law arises from the human capacity to respond to the truths of the natural law that are knowable through general and special revelation.[35] As put by VanDrunen: "The created world offers testimony to God and his law, and the human heart and conscience perceive them, respond to them, and make moral judgments accordingly. The natural order objectively communicates moral knowledge, and human beings are equipped to understand it subjectively (though they sinfully distort it)."[36]

Because the goodness of human life is a self-evident truth, "any sane person is capable of seeing that life, knowledge, fellowship, offspring," and other aspects of human existence are good and worth having.[37] Humans are not "empty vessels" when it comes to moral knowledge: The revealed law does not

32. Gifford Grobien, "What Is the Natural Law? Medieval Foundations and Luther's Appropriation," in *Natural Law: A Lutheran Reappraisal*, ed. Robert C. Baker (Concordia Publishing House, 2011), 21.

33. George, "Natural Law, God and Human Dignity," 57–59.

34. Calvin, *Institutes of the Christian Religion*, 1.5.18.

35. Walker, *Faithful Reason*, 125.

36. VanDrunen, *Divine Covenants and Moral Order*, 254.

37. Finnis, *Natural Law and Natural Rights*, 30.

"come as a bolt out of the blue with no discernible connection with what our minds can recognize as good."[38]

Through sin, "lewd and wicked custom," and neglect, our understanding of the moral law is defective, and needs correction through instruction and reading Scripture.[39] It is a long-standing element of Christian teaching that conscience is "a faculty that needs to be formed, trained, or developed rather than to be taken as found."[40] The Bible envisages a process of training in wisdom and the precepts of the moral law as we listen, meditate on the Word, and experience life in the world. We need to be instructed in wisdom and the precepts of the law (Prov. 2:1–6).

J. Budziszewski has helpfully described several "witnesses" to the natural law, which are means by which the natural law is promulgated.[41] These do not prove the existence of the natural law but bear witness to its truth. One witness, already mentioned above, is conscience, which Budziszewski calls the "interior witness to the foundational principles of moral law."[42] As affirmed in scriptural passages such as Romans 2:14–15, the work of the law is written on the heart and this interior light bears witness to the truth of the moral law. Conscience manifests itself in warning us against committing moral wrong and accusing us when we sin. Although it can be suppressed and seared, conscience can never be fully erased. To the extent

38. Budziszewski, *Companion to the Commentary*, 5.

39. Hooker, *Laws*, 1:67 [1.8.11]; Gerson Moreno-Riaño and Cary J. Nederman, "Marsilius of Padua's Principles of Secular Politics," in *A Companion to Marsilius of Padua*, ed. Gerson Moreno-Riaño and Cary J. Nederman (Brill, 2012), 121–22.

40. Ian Leigh, "Freedom of Conscience: Freedom of Conscience Assessing the Christian Contribution," in *Christianity and Constitutionalism*, ed. Nicholas Aroney and Ian Leigh (Oxford University Press, 2022), 291.

41. Budziszewski, *What We Can't Not Know*, chs. 4, 5, and 7; Budziszewski, *Commentary on Thomas Aquinas's Treatise on Law*, 224–27, 242.

42. Budziszewski, *What We Can't Not Know*, 85. Budziszewski distinguishes between "deep conscience" (*synderesis*) and "surface conscience" (*conscientia*).

that our knowledge of the moral law is defective, this is willful suppression rather than total ignorance.

The second witness is design, including the fact that we have been made in the image of God with a longing to know him, and features of human nature such as human sociability (the need to live in community with other people), the complementarity of male and female, and subsidiarity.

The third witness is the witness of consequences. As discussed in the previous chapter, transgressing the moral law brings consequences. These consequences provide evidence of both the existence of the moral law and its inherent connection with human nature.

Although many people may profess to believe that truth (especially moral truth) is relative, this is not, in reality, what we think or how we live. We are outraged at those who abuse women or children. We are angry at those who steal our property or cheat the elderly out of their life savings. We condemn corrupt governments that murder their opponents. We distrust liars and do not wish to be thought of as dishonest. We mourn the history of slavery and colonial oppression. We condemn the Holocaust, as well as murderers, thieves, rapists, fascists, organized criminals, and drug cartels. We admire those who show courage and self-sacrifice. We praise public-spirited citizens and criticize unsociable behavior. We recognize that generosity is a good thing. These attitudes are "evidence of a remnant morality trying to surface."[43]

What has been said so far in this section reflects another important claim made by classical natural law theory—namely, that human inclinations "are rational and can be discovered by human reason." Indeed, the principles (or "precepts") of

43. Walker, *Faithful Reason*, 28.

the natural law are embedded in our human reason—they are "written on the heart"—so that we "can't not know" them.[44]

Still, for many Protestants, the idea of an ability to discern the truths of the moral law outside of Scripture seems to paint an overly optimistic picture of the ability of human reason to yield an accurate understanding of the moral law. It is obviously true that many people reason to incorrect views about morality. It is now necessary to discuss the impact of sin on our ability to know the natural law.

The Impact of Sin

Three things can be said about how sin affects our ability to discern the natural law. The first is that our *knowledge* of the natural law is indeed distorted. As a result of sin and the corruption of our reason, humans are no longer able to understand or know the truth about God "except in an extremely dim way."[45] As John Calvin puts it, although humans have an inbuilt desire to know the truth, "man's mind, because of its dullness, cannot hold to the right path, but wanders through various errors and stumbles repeatedly as if it were groping in darkness. . . . Thus it betrays how incapable it is of seeking and finding truth."[46] An accurate knowledge of God and the natural law is no longer possible; our understanding is distorted and in need of correction by Scripture, which is the authoritative revelation of the moral law.[47]

Although opponents of natural law commonly accuse its proponents of claiming that humans can gain an accurate understanding

44. Pearson, "Luther's Pragmatic Appropriation," 43.
45. Grobien, "What Is the Natural Law?,"33.
46. Calvin, *Institutes of the Christian Religion*, 2.2.12.
47. Junius, *Mosaic Polity*, 52–53.

of the moral law without the need of Scripture,[48] no genuinely Protestant account of natural law would affirm this. The Bible clearly teaches that our knowledge of the moral law is distorted by sin (Jer. 17:9; Rom. 1:18–23; Titus 1:15). It is not possible for people to develop an accurate and complete knowledge of the moral law without the corrective lenses of Scripture. The doctrine of natural law does not deny that the Bible is a necessary corrective.

Second, our *ability* to carry out the precepts of the moral law is marred. As a result of the fall, "all people in existence are corrupt, and so they are hostile to every good thing, and tend or incline to every sort of evil only."[49] Not only is our knowledge of the law corrupted, but our ability to carry out its precepts is corrupted. Righteousness is not attainable through the law, and so the natural law serves to condemn. A genuinely Protestant doctrine of natural law does not suggest that humans can work their way up to God by means of the natural knowledge of the moral law that remains after the corruption wrought by sin.

Third, the natural knowledge of the moral law is not totally effaced. It is true that, as Girolamo Zanchi writes, after the fall, "natural law was almost entirely blotted out as was any law that looks to God and the worship of him or to our neighbors and the just and fair relationship with them. The entire image of God that stands firm in justice and holiness was lost. People became completely blind in their minds, totally depraved in their hearts, and altogether corrupted."[50]

And yet there remains a "residue" of understanding and judgment in the human mind.[51] Thinkers in the natural law

48. See Henry, "Natural Law and a Nihilistic Culture," 54; Cornelius Van Til, *Christian Apologetics* (P&R Publishing, 1976), 52–53.

49. Den Boer and Faber, eds., *Synopsis of a Purer Theology*, 1:145.

50. Zanchi, *On the Law in General*, 12.

51. Calvin, *Institutes of the Christian Religion*, 2.2.12.

tradition typically argue that it is impossible not to know the primary precepts of the natural law, so that even habitual liars and thieves are aware that lying and theft are wrong. Augustine writes that "so powerful is the attraction of the virtue of purity that practically every human being is pleased to hear it praised, and no one is so sunk in depravity as to have lost all sense of decency."[52] Francisco Suárez writes that "it is not possible that one should in any way be ignorant of the primary principles of the natural law."[53] "Murder is wrong for everyone; moreover the wrong of murder is known to everyone."[54]

Aquinas says that "human reason could not go astray in the abstract, as to the universal principles of the natural law; but through being habituated to sin, it became obscured in the point of things to be done in detail" (*ST* I-II, 99.2). That is, all people know the universal principles of the moral law, even though we may have incorrect beliefs about how those principles apply in particular cases.[55]

Protestant thinkers, who are typically more pessimistic about the impact of sin, have made similar claims. Girolamo Zanchi writes that the natural law "is so impressed on the human heart that it cannot be altered by anyone or completely blotted out from the heart."[56] Martin Luther argues that "not an individual is there who does not realize, and who is not forced to confess, the justice and truth of the natural law outlined in the command"—namely, the Golden Rule.[57] Contemporary anthro-

52. Augustine, *The City of God Books I–VII*, trans. Demetrius B. Zema and Gerald G. Walsh (Catholic University of America Press, 1950), 121 [II.26].

53. Suárez, "A Treatise on Laws," 248, 300.

54. Budziszewski, *Treatise on Divine Law*, 55.

55. Budziszewski, *Treatise on Divine Law*, 55.

56. Zanchi, *On the Law in General*, 23. See also Hooker, *Laws*, 1:66 [1.8.9].

57. Martin Luther, "Sermon for the Fourth Sunday After Epiphany: Romans 13:8–10," in *Sermons of Martin Luther*, ed. John Nicholas Lenker (Baker, 1983), 7:73.

pological research supports this claim, with one writer arguing that "in all the great traditions, and probably in all cultures, we find conceptual equivalents of the 'golden rule' in the sense of 'do unto others as you would want them to do unto you.'"[58]

Even where people hold morally repugnant views, these are often perverted forms of the basic goods.[59] To take an example, many today defend the legitimacy of abortion. But people who defend abortion would likely not disagree with the principle that it is wrong to take innocent life. Instead, they would generally try to argue that the moral principle does not apply, arguing that abortion is not really *killing*, or that an unborn child is not really *innocent*, or is not *human*, or is not *life*.[60]

In recognizing the reality and limits of our natural knowledge of the moral law, Protestant thinkers have often argued that our natural knowledge of "civil" or earthly matters is less distorted than our knowledge of "sacred" matters.[61] Precisely how much "natural light" remains will vary, given that different peoples know the natural law to a greater or lesser extent.[62]

Calvin, for instance, distinguishes between knowledge of earthly things that pertain to this present life (such as matters of policy and economy, the mechanical arts, and liberal studies) and knowledge of heavenly things (such as the knowledge of God and his will, the mysteries of the heavenly kingdom, and the means of attaining true righteousness). We have already seen Calvin's pessimistic view about natural human ability to discern truths about heavenly things. With regard to earthly things, however, Calvin is much more optimistic: "Since man is

58. Antweiler, *Our Common Denominator*, 108.

59. Finnis, *Natural Law and Natural Rights*, 91.

60. Budziszewski, *What We Can't Not Know*, 168–70.

61. See also Marsilius of Padua, *Defensor Pacis*, trans. Alan Gewirth (Columbia University Press, 2001), 51.

62. Zanchi, *On the Law in General*, 21–22.

by nature a social animal, he tends through natural instinct to foster and preserve society. Consequently, we observe that there exist in all men's minds universal impressions of a certain civic fair dealing and order. Hence no man is to be found who does not understand that every sort of human organization must be regulated by laws, and who does not comprehend the principles of those laws. Hence arises that unvarying consent of all nations and of individual mortals with regard to laws. For their seeds have, without teacher or lawgiver, been implanted in all men."[63]

This distinction seems to be basically correct.[64] That is, sin distorts our knowledge of the natural law and our ability to carry out the precepts of the moral law. As to matters of salvation and the knowledge of God's character, humans are blind unless instructed by Scripture. However, in earthly and civil matters there remains some knowledge of the moral law, which explains things such as general human honesty and decency. As put by Herman Bavinck: "In spiritual, heavenly matters, knowledge, will, and ability have been entirely lost. In moral and civil matters, in temporal, earthly matters, knowledge, will, and ability have been weakened, but not entirely taken away. There is therefore a certain good, measured by an earthly, temporal standard—and by natural persons themselves—that acquires temporal rewards. In themselves those virtues are good. But evaluated by the measure of God's holiness, the best virtues are splendid vices."[65]

Scripture is thus necessary to correct our faulty understanding of things that we have always known, but never truly known: "Revelation catches man out in the guilty possession

63. Calvin, *Institutes of the Christian Religion*, 2.2.13.

64. Stephen K. Moroney agrees but also considers the distinction to be "insufficiently precise": *The Noetic Effects of Sin: A Historical and Contemporary Exploration of How Sin Affects Our Thinking* (Lexington Books, 2000), 14.

65. Herman Bavinck, *Reformed Ethics: Created, Fallen, and Converted Humanity*, ed. John Bolt (Baker Academic, 2019), 1:161.

of a knowledge which he has always had, but from which he has never won a true understanding."[66]

Prudence and Practical Reason

Sometimes natural law is thought of as a rule book or code of behavior.[67] It is of course true, as I have discussed, that there are moral rules and absolutes. But I have also emphasized that the moral order is broader than simply a list of rules and precepts. In addition, I have argued that there is a level of vagueness to the moral order and that there is an intermediate category between morally binding and morally neutral. God's law in the Bible is often quite open-textured, consisting of broad guiding principles rather than a detailed code of practice.[68] Moral reasoning in Proverbs is not primarily "the application of absolute laws or rigid doctrine," but rather allows space for indeterminacy, recognizing that it is not possible to lay down rigid a priori rules that apply in all cases.[69]

Natural law is not a rule book that gives tidy answers for all of life's questions. Rather, natural law sets out foundational principles of wisdom and reason that reflect the created moral order and that need to be implemented in concrete ways in particular situations. Living wisely requires wisdom—namely, "a practical knowledge of how to act well, grounded in the reality of the world God has made."[70]

66. O'Donovan, *Resurrection and Moral Order*, 89.

67. See e.g., Joseph R. Biden Jr., "Law and Natural Law: Questions for Judge Thomas," *Washington Post*, September 8, 1991.

68. Packer, "Conscience, Choice and Character," ed. Bruce Kaye and Gordon Wenham, 180.

69. Anne W. Stewart, *Poetic Ethics in Proverbs: Wisdom Literature and the Shaping of the Moral Self* (Cambridge University Press, 2016), 175, 182.

70. Errington, *Every Good Path*, 3.

As mentioned earlier in this chapter, the foundational precepts of the natural law (outlined in chapter 3) are often referred to as the primary precepts of practical reason. Practical reason is reasoning directed to action, and it is implemented when deliberating about the most effective means to achieve a desired end. That is, it seeks to determine the right course of action in the particular circumstances, rather than seeking understanding of the way things are (which is often referred to as *speculative reason*).

This requires the virtue of prudence, which Aquinas defined as "right reason applied to action" (*ST* II-II, 47.2). Prudence means deliberating about "the means of obtaining a due end": Where there is more than one legitimate means of obtaining an end, prudence must be exercised.[71] Prudence is the virtue that perceives the human goods as goods and translates the unchangeable standards of justice into concrete proposals.[72]

Prudence is necessary because often there will not be one single way of acting on the principles of the natural law. For example, there is no one single way to apply the precept that one should give generously out of one's superfluous possessions. Merely identifying something as a good is not enough. There are principles of wisdom as to how and when we pursue those goods. The goods may conflict with each other, and humans have limited capacity, so we cannot pursue all the goods all the time. We ought not to pursue one thing excessively to the exclusion of other goods. We will typically need to pursue the goods in moderation. With the exception of our duty to worship and obey the one true God, none of the goods are absolute.

71. Aquinas, *ST* II-II, 47.10; Russell Hittinger, *The First Grace: Rediscovering the Natural Law in a Post-Christian World* (ISI Books, 2007), xliv.

72. Oderberg, *Moral Theory*, 51; Marsilius of Padua, *Defensor Pacis*, 1.13.8; Cary J. Nederman, *Community and Consent: The Secular Political Theory of Marsiglio of Padua's Defensor Pacis* (Rowman & Littlefield, 1995), 58, 78, 82.

Determining how and when to pursue the goods of natural law is a matter of prudence and practical reason. This means that there is a level of uncertainty in practical reasoning. Implementing the foundational principles of natural law will depend on the circumstances, which will vary.[73]

Development in Natural Law Principles

Christians typically resist the idea that the natural law is changeable. The moral law is based on the character of God and human nature, and God does not change.[74] And yet, it seems that there has been development in moral principles. For example, a variety of moral and legal principles have been developed that are now treated as normative in the Western legal tradition, including principles of constitutionalism that constrain and limit civil government.

Under the principle of the rule of law, all people are subject to the law, including civil rulers themselves. The principle of the separation of powers stipulates that power ought to be divided among different branches of government. Judicial independence requires that judges be protected from interference from the executive branch, and so have security of tenure and remuneration. Representative government requires that government officials be elected by and accountable to the people. Due process requires that all government decisions be made according to a fair process, especially that a person adversely affected by a decision be given an opportunity to be heard before a decision is made.[75]

73. See e.g., Budziszewski, *Treatise on Divine Law*, 55.

74. See Grotius, *The Rights of War and Peace*, 1:155–6.

75. Finnis, *Natural Law and Natural Rights*, 288, lists a number of other principles that are desirable in any stable legal system.

These principles are not typically thought to be directly contained in the natural law. As such, they are probably not binding on all people at all times. For instance, it was not wrong for King Solomon to make judicial determinations in his capacity as king (1 Kings 3:16–28), but this would not be considered appropriate today. In earlier generations, a stable body of tenured judges did not exist, and the distinction between legislative, executive, and judicial power was much less pronounced.

And yet, there is something normative about these principles, such that civil regimes that do not operate consistently with those principles are rightly considered defective. Now that the principles of constitutionalism have been derived or concluded, there is no going back: Governments should only act in accordance with the law; government officials today should be elected by and accountable to the people, and civil governments should create an independent body of tenured judges.

How then can we account for the development of key principles such as those outlined above while also acknowledging that God's character does not change?

The principles I have mentioned can be seen as the outworking of natural law principles, and these conclusions are valid by virtue of the principles.[76] That is, in the natural law there is a core idea of, for example, justice, and these principles flesh out what is necessary to give effect to that core principle. Judicial independence and the separation of powers are not ends in themselves but designed to secure accountability and good government. A judge who is not independent could nevertheless render a just judgment, and a nonrepresentative monarch could make a wise decision.

76. Junius, *Mosaic Polity*, 85.

John of Salisbury writes that "every magistrate is the servant of justice" and that justice must not be offered for sale.[77] Therefore, judges should be placed in a position where they are protected from the temptation to do so. Therefore, judges should be independent; they should have security of tenure and be well remunerated. Of these propositions, only the first, "it is wrong to sell injustice," is universal. The others follow by deduction or conclusion from this principle. They flesh out what is necessary to ensure that justice is impartial and have normative force but are not universally binding.

Scripture contemplates that ruler and ruled alike are subject to the law (Deut. 17:18–20), which can be seen as an embryonic statement of the rule of law. Modern theorists have argued that the rule of law requires (among other things) that legal rules be prospective, promulgated, clear, stable, and relatively general and not impossible to comply with.[78] These requirements flesh out what is required to give effect to the core principle.

Discrimination on ethnic or racial grounds would not have been considered wrong by many thinkers in earlier generations. But discrimination is rightly considered to be wrong now, as a deduction from principles of the natural law, especially human dignity and the Golden Rule.

These principles can be seen as a kind of change in the natural law: "The foundations of natural law cannot change, but new secondary precepts may acquire the force of natural law on the basis of the general precepts."[79] That is, by virtue of the foundational principles of the natural law, conclusions such as

77. John of Salisbury, *Policraticus*, ed. Cary J. Nederman (Cambridge University Press, 2011), 93–94, 135.

78. Finnis, *Natural Law and Natural Rights*, 273.

79. Budziszewski, *Treatise on Law*, 301.

the rule of law and the wrongness of discrimination are now considered to have normative force.

Some Examples of Natural Law Reasoning

How might a robust doctrine of natural law assist Christians in thinking about difficult questions? This section takes some examples to illustrate the benefits of a natural law approach to moral reasoning. We will start with a handful of comparatively trivial issues.[80]

Beauty. Protestant Christians are often suspicious of beauty and the pursuit of beauty. And, of course, in today's world beauty is often idolized and distorted. However, beauty is a good thing, and even necessary to understand God. Jonathan Edwards wrote that "God is God, and distinguished from all other Beings, and exalted above them, chiefly by his divine Beauty, which is infinitely diverse from all other Beauty."[81] Natural law theorists have argued that beauty, or aesthetic experience, is a self-evident and noninstrumental good, something worth pursuing for its own sake.[82] This is so if beauty in the world is a type of the divine beauty and reveals something of the Creator.[83] There appears to be something inherently human about appreciating beauty and creating beautiful things.

Sports, play, and competitiveness. Sports may seem a trivial issue, but it is an obvious and pervasive feature of human societies. Given the hours spent by many people engaging in (and

80. Other examples could be given, such as friendship, art, literature, music, poetry, and symbolism.

81. Jonathan Edwards, *A Treatise Concerning Religious Affections* (Boston: printed for S. Kneeland and T. Green, 1746), 188.

82. Crowe, *Natural Law and the Nature of Law*, 50–51; Finnis, *Natural Law and Natural Rights*, 87–88.

83. McDermott, *Everyday Glory*, 55–56.

watching) sports, it is worth reflecting on. Jonathan Crowe has argued that play, especially structured forms of engagement that contain internal standards of excellence, is a basic human good and that engaging in forms of play such as sports is intelligible without the need for further explanation.[84] Sport can be seen as a good, albeit a non-absolute one.

Exercise and nutrition. Exercise and nutrition cannot affect a person's salvation, but they can obviously have a significant impact on health and well-being. Scripture has almost nothing to say about exercise, which means that discussions of exercise among Christians typically revolve around a single verse: 1 Timothy 4:8 ("While bodily training is of some value, godliness is of value in every way, as it holds promise for the present life and also for the life to come"). As with exercise, nutrition is something that Protestants seem to have difficulty thinking about well. Many Christians seemingly have little regard for good nutrition while others are tempted to turn the Bible into a handbook for eating, arguing for example that we should follow the Old Testament food laws or Daniel's vegetables-only diet today.[85] Both approaches are a recipe for disaster.

Can natural law shed any light on the subject? The first precept of the natural law is that life is a good and that people should seek their own conservation. Eating a nutritious diet so as to maintain your body in good health is an obvious deduction to draw from this principle. Precisely what such a diet consists of will depend on a range of things, including cost and availability, and is not prescribed by Scripture. While fitness and health are relative goods and should not become idols, it is widely acknowledged that exercise brings many benefits such as increased energy and strength.

84. Crowe, *Natural Law and the Nature of Law*, 48–49.

85. E.g., Elizabeth Snyder, "Biblical Foundations for Nutrition and an Abundant Life," *Journal of Biblical Foundations of Faith and Learning* 1, no. 1 (2016).

Education. Scripture has little to say about education. As a result, Protestants typically reason poorly about it, being tempted to reduce it to teaching about God or skills and character training. Considering education through the lens of natural law can help resolve many of the problems that Protestants face when thinking about education. A natural law approach recognizes that knowledge is a self-evident good, given the nature of humans as rational beings.[86] Knowledge is inherently worth pursuing for its own sake.

Aquinas notes that "'those things which nature has taught to all animals' are said to belong to the natural law, such as the union of male and female and the education of the young and similar things" (*ST* I-II, 94.2). Protestant writers have argued along similar lines.[87] That is, it is an obvious feature of the world that children are born in need of care and instruction and so parents have a duty to educate and raise their children. Scripture, perhaps, does not address this because it is such an obvious truth that does not need emphasizing. Scripture gives general principles for raising children, but there are many details not included.

Husbands and wives. Peter instructs husbands to live with their wives in an understanding way (1 Pet. 3:7). This reflects the reality that men and women are different, and so, in order to follow this injunction, husbands must understand something of those differences. Some are described in Scripture, but it is also necessary to learn from observation and experience.[88] That is, what precisely husbands must do to fulfill this injunction requires an understanding of the differences between men and women, which must be illuminated by experience. Natural law, therefore,

86. Finnis, *Natural Law and Natural Rights*, 64–65.

87. E.g., Bullinger, *The Decades of Henry Bullinger*, 1:291–94.

88. See, for example, Shaunti and Jeff Feldhahn, *For Men Only: A Straightforward Guide to the Inner Lives of Women* (Multnomah Books, 2013).

helps flesh out the meaning of the scriptural command in a way that would be inadequate were we to rely solely on Scripture.

Gambling. Most Christians consider gambling to be wrong, or at least unwise. And yet while there are relevant biblical principles,[89] gambling is not specifically addressed one way or the other in Scripture. Natural law teaches that acting wisely means conforming to the moral order inscribed in creation. Gambling almost invariably results in financial losses, and addiction can have serious consequences for people and their families. While gambling is not specifically condemned by Scripture, it is widely recognized to be harmful.

Drugs. The Bible includes teaching about alcohol but does not specifically address smoking or the use of drugs. Drugs are expensive, illegal in many countries, have harmful health effects, and readily lead to addiction. This suggests that the use of drugs is wrong, or at the very least extremely unwise.

Sociability. Natural law theorists have argued that humans have a natural inclination to live in society, and natural law includes the precept that we should, in Aquinas's words, "avoid giving offence to those among whom one has to live" (*ST* I-II, 94.2). A recent case from the Federal Court of Australia provides an interesting illustration of this point. Two neighbors had a protracted dispute involving multiple court proceedings. In handing down his ruling, the judge expressed a hope that the decision would bring the dispute to an end, including the following comments, which seem to me to illustrate Aquinas's point well: "It is to be hoped that, in the future, [the two neighbours] will find the means to forbear. When it comes to neighbours, it

89. Relevant scriptural principles include warnings against the love of money, the assertion that the building of wealth comes through hard work, and the need for contentment: e.g., Prov. 13:11; 28:19; Eccles. 5:10; Matt. 6:24; Luke 12:15; 1 Tim. 6:9–10; Heb. 13:5.

is better to withdraw than to offend. Certainly it is best to avoid abusive language of any kind. In their own shared interests, I encourage them both to draw a line and begin again."[90]

Much more could be said about these questions. All I hope to have accomplished in this section is to provide some illustrative examples of how adopting a natural law approach can expand our moral vocabulary and enable a more nuanced discussion of important issues.

Two Controversial Questions

Let us now consider two contentious examples. The first is contraception. The Roman Catholic Church considers that the natural law prohibits the use of contraception, teaching that "every action which, whether in anticipation of the conjugal act, or in its accomplishment, or in the development of its natural consequences, proposes, whether as an end or as a means, to render procreation impossible" is intrinsically evil.[91]

Does accepting the doctrine of natural law mean that we are bound to accept that contraception is wrong? Some Protestant writers do consider that contraception is wrong or at least problematic.[92] Many, however, would resist such an approach on the basis that it is not specifically prohibited by Scripture, and so this is an unwarranted imposition on people's consciences.[93]

In my opinion, a natural law approach provides a valuable framework for thinking through the question. Natural law invites us to a more nuanced discussion than simply whether

90. Bharatiya v. Antonio [2022] FCA 428 [71].

91. *Catechism of the Catholic Church*, 570 [2370].

92. E.g., Walker, *Faithful Reason*, 309–12.

93. This is a comparatively recent view: Matthew Lee Anderson, "Procreation and Children," in *Protestant Social Teaching: An Introduction*, ed. Onsi Aaron Kamel et al. (Davenant Institute, 2022).

there is a Bible verse prohibiting contraception. Natural law teaches that there is a moral order that does not always yield one-size-fits-all answers to difficult questions. In short, natural law orients the question as one of wisdom.

Scripture indeed does not directly prohibit contraception. It presents children and family as blessings and good things (Gen. 1:28; Ps. 127:3–5). Natural law theorists have recognized that procreation and marriage are self-evident goods and that humans have a natural inclination to unite sexually and reproduce.[94] Fertility and reproduction are good and beautiful things.[95] But they are not absolute goods. In my opinion, this issue can be seen as falling into an intermediate category between morally binding and morally neutral: Marriage and procreation are good things that we ought to seek, but there is no specific precept or rule that we should marry, and no obligation to pursue these goods all the time.[96]

The fact that Scripture does not prohibit contraception should not be the end of the matter. Approaching contraception as a matter of natural law would direct us to consider the ends and purposes of human sexuality. While reproduction must obviously be given a central place, children are not the primary object of attention in the marriage relationship or its sole focus, and the production of children is not the sole object of human sexuality.[97]

A natural law approach also directs us to consider the implications for individuals and society. Several authors have powerfully argued that contraception has effected a fundamental change in the nature of what it means to be a person, with

94. Aquinas, *ST* I-II, 94.2; Finnis, *Natural Law and Natural Rights*, 86–90; Walker, *Faithful Reason*, 163–65; Crowe, *Natural Law and the Nature of Law*, 35.

95. Favale, *Genesis of Gender*, 92, 100.

96. Aquinas, *ST* II-II, 152.2.

97. Oliver O'Donovan, *Begotten or Made?* (Clarendon Press, 1984), 17.

hugely significant—and highly problematic—consequences for society. Abigail Favale argues that "the unmooring of sex from life has cheapened it and cheapened us, fueling a consumerist sexual paradigm that trumpets liberation while enslaving us," as well as pathologizing the healthy functioning of the female body.[98] In similar terms Mary Harrington argues that contraception is part of a cultural development that sees the human body as something to be controlled and manipulated, rather than something that defines us.[99]

If correct, this suggests that, while contraception might not be sinful, it also may not be generally good for society. The point of this is not to arrogate the power to lay down extrabiblical requirements and prescriptions. Christ remains lord of the conscience. Instead, it is to invite us to consider the consequences of where our technologies and practices are taking us. Contraception is an illustration of the point that things that are not in the category of right and wrong may nevertheless be more or less wise.

A second example is in vitro fertilization (IVF), the conception of children by harvesting female eggs and fertilizing them outside the body and then implanting the fertilized eggs in a woman's uterus. As with contraception, the Roman Catholic Church has no doubts about the morality of such practices: "Techniques that entail the dissociation of husband and wife, by the intrusion of a person other than the couple (donation of sperm or ovum, surrogate uterus), are gravely immoral. These techniques (heterologous artificial insemination and fertilization) infringe the child's right to be born of a father and mother known to him and bound to each other by marriage. They betray the spouses' 'right to become a father and a mother only through each other.'"[100]

98. Favale, *Genesis of Gender*, 107.
99. Mary Harrington, *Feminism Against Progress* (Regnery Publishing, 2023).
100. *Catechism of the Catholic Church*, 571 [2376].

How might a distinctly Protestant account of natural law approach this issue? Some Protestants agree that IVF is clearly wrong. Andrew Walker argues on natural law grounds that IVF "is not an ethical practice" because it violates the "sacrosanct and inviolable principle of conception resulting from the bodily union of husband and wife."[101] As with contraception, I argue that natural law orients the question as one of wisdom, which directs us to, among other things, the consequences of IVF. And those consequences are profound. As the Roman Catholic Church has recognized, IVF dissociates the sexual act from the procreative act: "The act which brings the child into existence is no longer an act by which two persons give themselves to one another, but one that 'entrusts the life and identity of the embryo into the power of doctors and biologists and establishes the domination of technology over the origin and destiny of the human person.'"[102]

IVF brings the creation of life within the realm of human artifice and renders it a product of the human will. And if the creation of life is subject to technological manipulation, what is exempt? The only limit on human power is the limit of technological advancement. If the legitimacy of IVF is granted, it is impossible to resist the extension of the logic of human plasticity to other areas, from abortion to transgender ideology.

These are not issues that just concern the church: All people should rightly be fearful about untrammeled technological advancement and the redefinition of human nature. As C. S. Lewis recognized, "What we call Man's power over Nature turns out to be a power exercised by some men over other men with Nature as its instrument."[103] It can only exacerbate the tendency

101. Walker, *Faithful Reason*, 279–82.
102. *Catechism of the Catholic Church*, 571 [2377].
103. Lewis, *Abolition of Man*, 40.

to enable public authorities to intervene in the most intimate features of human existence.[104]

Few Protestants seem willing to confront the nature of these technologies and their implications. While we ought to be cautious before imposing a new command to the effect that "you must not conceive children by IVF," a natural law perspective would urge caution regarding IVF.

Conclusion

A common Protestant fear is that natural law has the effect of giving license to the church to impose human-made rules and restrictions on Christians that are not found in Scripture. And, of course, God alone is lord of the conscience.[105] What I have sought to show in this chapter is that natural law is not a rule book or code of behavior imposing extrabiblical requirements. Rather, it is an invitation to wisdom, to broaden our moral vocabulary and to consider the richness of the created order in all its complexity. Rather than having separate silos of Bible for the church and reason for our secular lives, natural law helps integrate "secular" and "biblical" reasoning into a harmonious whole. As Hooker wrote, that which guides and directs our reason is the general law of nature, "which law of nature and the moral law of Scripture are in the substance of law all one."[106]

If natural law can inform human reason even post-fall, how should it affect institutions other than the church, like civil government?

104. Pope Paul VI, *Humanae Vitae* (July 25, 1968), [17], [23].

105. *WCF* 20.2; Charles Hodge, *Systematic Theology* (Charles Scribner & Co., 1872), 1:183 ("The people of God are bound by nothing but the Word of God").

106. Hooker, *Laws*, 1:167 [3.9.2].

6

Natural Law and Civil Law

There is a long tradition of thinking about civil government and civil law from a natural law perspective. This chapter explores the relationship between natural law and human civil law—that is, laws enacted by civil governments. It discusses how natural law provides the foundation for civil government and the foundational principles for civil law. The Christian tradition has long argued that natural law provides the foundation for human civil law. Natural law is also a standard against which positive law can be evaluated.

Natural Law and Civil Government

Natural law theorists have widely argued that natural law provides the foundation for civil government. Passages in Proverbs view government as deriving its authority from being ordained within the created order.[1] An enduring strand of thinking in

1. Bartholomew, "A Time for War," 105, referring to Proverbs 8:15–16, among other passages.

the Christian tradition argues that humans have been made as inherently social and political creatures, with a need for society and political organization. It is thus a widespread feature of human communities that political structures are formed to regulate common life. This recognizes that there are important human goods that can only be realized through the institutions of human civil law and government: "A justly ordered society is a requirement of human nature if human beings are to survive, let alone flourish."[2]

Aristotle famously wrote that "man is by nature a political animal."[3] Many thinkers in the Christian tradition have echoed this idea. Aquinas writes that "it is natural for man, more than for any other animal, to be a social and political animal, to live in a group."[4] John of Paris argues that civil government "derives from natural law in that man is a civil or political and social animal."[5] Similar comments could be cited from a host of authors.[6] Writers within the Reformed tradition have expressed similar views. Calvin argues that "since man is by nature a social animal, he tends through natural instinct to

2. David Novak, *Natural Law in Judaism* (Cambridge University Press, 1998), 36; Finnis, *Natural Law and Natural Rights*, 3.

3. Aristotle, *Politics*, trans. T. A. Sinclair and Trevor J. Saunders (Penguin Books, 1981) 1.2, 1253a1.

4. Aquinas, *On Kingship*, 4.

5. John of Paris, *On Royal and Papal Power*, trans. J. A. Watt (Pontifical Institute of Mediaeval Studies, 1971), 79.

6. Lactantius, *The Divine Institutes*, 417–18 [VI.10]; Dante Alighieri, *Il Convivio (The Banquet)*, trans. Richard H. Lansing (Garland Library of Medieval Literature, 1990), 4.4, https://digitaldante.columbia.edu/text/library/the-convivio/book-04/#04; Giles of Rome, *The Governance of Kings and Princes: John Trevisa's Middle English Translation of the De Regimine Principum of Aegidius Romanus*, ed. David C. Fowler, Charles F. Briggs, and Paul G. Remley (Garland, 1997), 287; James of Viterbo, *De Regimine Christiano: A Critical Edition and Translation*, trans. R. W. Dyson (Brill, 2009), 9 [1.1]; Francisco de Vitoria, "On Civil Power," in *Political Writings*, ed. Anthony Pagden (Cambridge University Press, 1991), 6–9; Fortescue, *On the Laws and Governance of England*, 132; Suárez, "A Treatise on Laws," 52.

foster and preserve society" and that the seeds of civil law and government "have, without teacher or lawgiver, been implanted in all men."[7]

Civil government reflects this basic human tendency: A universal feature of human life is that people unite together in social and political groupings and structure those groupings with rule and leadership.[8] Civil government serves important purposes such as peace, political order, and justice, which could not otherwise be obtained.[9]

However, natural law theorists have recognized that there is no one divinely prescribed form of government that people must adhere to. The precise form of civil government is, therefore, a matter for human choice and decision.[10] Humans have an inherent need to form social and political communities, and it is a requirement of natural reasonableness that there be a governmental authority.[11] The law of nature requires that political authority of some sort be established, but the form of government established in any polity is something to be determined by the people.[12]

A different stream of thought within the Christian tradition, typically traced back to Augustine,[13] argues that political authority is a remedy for sin and would not have existed if there had been no fall. Abraham Kuyper, for instance, argues that

7. Calvin, *Institutes of the Christian Religion*, 2.2.13. See also Hooker, *Laws*, 1:70 [1.10.1]; Melanchthon, *Chief Theological Topics*, 44; Hemmingsen, *On the Law of Nature*, 103.

8. Suárez, "A Treatise on Laws," 419–22, 432.

9. Hemmingsen, *On the Law of Nature*, 80.

10. Suárez, "A Treatise on Laws," 441–42.

11. Finnis, *Natural Law and Natural Rights*, 248.

12. Knud Haakonssen, *Natural Law and Moral Philosophy: From Grotius to the Scottish Enlightenment* (Cambridge University Press, 1996), 17.

13. St. Augustine, *Concerning the City of God Against the Pagans*, trans. Henry Bettenson (Penguin Books, 1972), 19.15, 19.17.

"sin alone has necessitated the institution of governments" and that "neither bar of justice nor police, nor army, nor navy, is conceivable in a world without sin."[14]

Civil government certainly plays an important role in punishing evil and restraining sin (Rom. 13:1–7). It is also true that there are indications in Scripture of government and rule prior to the fall, and it seems to me to be accurate to say that government arises out of the inherently social and political nature of humans.[15] As I have argued elsewhere in this book, the original creation order remains normative, and so there are important areas of continuity between the pre- and postlapsarian states.

Natural law also has a distinctive view in elaborating the purpose and function of civil government. Natural law theorists argue that the role of civil law and government is to promote the common good. According to the classical legal tradition, civil government should be a "reasoned ordering to the common good."[16] The common good is "the flourishing of a well-ordered community,"[17] consisting of "a state of affairs where all agents (or, on some accounts, all members of a given community) are able to participate in the basic goods in a range of reasonable ways."[18] That is, the common good aims to secure the conditions necessary for people to flourish by acting in common.

14. Abraham Kuyper, *Lectures on Calvinism* (Eerdmans, 1931), 80, 83.

15. David C. Innes, *Christ and the Kingdoms of Men: Foundations of Political Life* (P&R Publishing, 2019), ch. 3.

16. Adrian Vermeule, *Common Good Constitutionalism* (Polity Press, 2022), 1.

17. Vermeule, *Common Good Constitutionalism*, 7; see also George Duke, "The Principle of the Common Good," in *Christianity and Global Law*, ed. Rafael Domingo and John Witte Jr. (Routledge, 2020).

18. Jonathan Crowe, "Natural Law Beyond Finnis," *American Journal of Jurisprudence* 2 (2011): 293, 301.

Natural Law and Civil Law

Natural law also provides the foundation for human civil law. Natural law provides an objective standard against which to measure human law. As Cicero famously said, "If justice were determined by popular vote or by the decrees of princes or the decisions of judges, then it would be just to commit highway robbery or adultery or to forge wills, if such things were approved by popular vote."[19] A natural law approach argues that there are inherent limits on the power of civil government.

Thinkers in the Christian tradition have almost universally held that natural law is the source of all valid human laws: All human law must be enacted by a lawful authority and based on the natural law. As Girolamo Zanchi writes, "Right and just laws are those conceived by those who have authority, are derived from natural or divine law, and exist for the good and well-being of the State or the church."[20] Franciscus Junius argues that human laws derive from the natural law. Human laws make determinations from the natural law in particular circumstances.[21]

Some definitions will be useful at this point. Thomas Aquinas famously defined law as an "ordinance of reason for the common good, made and promulgated by him who has care of the community" (*ST* I-II, 90.4). Aquinas distinguished four different types of law: eternal law, natural law, human law, and divine law (*ST* I-II, 91.1–4). The natural law is the unchangeable and universally applicable moral law, applicable to all humans (which Aquinas saw as a participation in the eternal law). Divine law, the specific commands given in Scripture, help to clarify the content of the natural law. Positive laws are temporal

19. Cicero, *On the Commonwealth and On the Laws*, 2nd ed., trans. and ed. James E. G. Zetzel (Cambridge University Press, 2017), 123.
20. Zanchi, *On the Law in General*, 4–5, 27.
21. Junius, *Mosaic Polity*, 54–55.

laws, made by a particular authority at a particular time, as an application of the natural law.

Human civil laws and ecclesiastical laws are both examples of positive law. Divine law given by God in Scripture for particular purposes (such as the Mosaic laws) are also examples of positive laws—namely, divine positive laws, intended to regulate, for example, specific aspects of the life of Israel as God's covenant people.

In order to be considered legitimate, human positive laws must be based on and consistent with the principles of the natural law. This is the constructive function of the natural law—that is, providing "a guide for the formulation of laws to promote the common good."[22] Civil laws must be an "ordinance of reason for the common good." In addition, civil laws must be "made and promulgated by him who has care of the community." The primary way of creating civil laws is enactment by a lawfully constituted authority—namely, those entrusted with the task of making laws within a given polity such as the legislature.[23]

Although they are constrained by the natural law, lawmakers have considerable freedom when enacting civil laws. One reason for this is that the natural law is relatively indeterminate: It sets out general principles rather than the precise way they are to be implemented in each situation. A second reason for this is that law is highly dependent on the circumstances. For both these reasons it is impossible to frame one changeless set of human civil laws that apply universally throughout history.[24]

While the natural law does not change, human laws "cannot be eternal and unchangeable because their circumstances can

22. Rice, *Fifty Questions*, 62.

23. Zanchi, *On the Law in General*, 5, 27; Junius, *Mosaic Polity*, 40; Hooker, *Laws*, 1:75 [1.10.8]; Finnis, *Natural Law and Natural Rights*, 27.

24. Junius, *Mosaic Polity*, 30 (thesis 10); Hemmingsen, *On the Law of Nature*, 161.

change."[25] As Aquinas writes, "The general principles of the natural law cannot be applied to all men in the same way because of the great variety of human circumstances; and hence arises the diversity of positive laws among various people" (*ST* I-II, 95.2). Human civil laws apply the principles of the natural law in a variable and contextual manner, and so are subject to change.[26]

It is therefore helpful to think of the natural law as the foundation: It provides the bedrock principles that ought to underlie civil law, but not the detail necessary for a system of human law. Civil lawmakers enjoy the creative freedom of an architect.[27] Lawmakers ought to promote the values enshrined in the moral law, but there is freedom, and the need for wisdom, in determining how to go about doing this.

Natural law provides the foundational, self-evident principles of morality, and civil laws implement the principles of the natural law in particular contexts. How, precisely, do civil laws do this?

How Positive Laws Give Effect to the Natural Law

Human positive laws determine the particular arrangements by which society shall be governed, drawing on the precepts of the natural law. Aquinas writes that "human reason must necessarily proceed to derive from the precepts of the natural law, as from general and indemonstrable principles, certain arrangements of a more particular kind. And these particular arrangements, devised by human reason, are called human laws, provided that the other conditions belonging to the character of law are present" (*ST* I-II, 91.3).

25. Zanchi, *On the Law in General*, 38.
26. Junius, *Mosaic Polity*, 15–18, 66, 88, 95–96, 109, 114.
27. Finnis, *Natural Law and Natural Rights*, 28.

Protestant writers and confessions contemplate something similar. For instance, the *Westminster Confession of Faith* states that the Old Testament judicial laws have expired and do not now need to be obeyed "further than the general equity thereof may require" (*WCF* 19.4). This seems to envisage a process of determining the universally applicable principles of the natural law that are embodied in the judicial laws and applying those principles in today's context. On the Reformed account, the law of Moses is a perfect exemplar of human law, providing a model for how human civil laws should relate to the natural law. Junius wrote that the laws of Moses did not simply derive from the law of nature but were "accommodated to human and political conditions."[28]

Thinkers within the classical natural law tradition have argued that civil laws relate to the natural law by making determinations of the natural law, additions to the natural law, and issuing punishments in accordance with the natural law. We will look at each of these in turn.

Determination. Civil laws provide determinations of the natural law.[29] A determination specifies details that natural law leaves indeterminate. A determination is where the universal principles of the moral law do not mandate one particular course of action, and so several ways of doing things are compatible with the natural law. Human civil laws "determine many points which have not been determined by the natural or the divine law, and which were not capable of being suitably determined by them."[30]

This will often be the case because the natural law gives the general principles rather than the details of their application

28. Junius, *Mosaic Polity*, 62.
29. Zanchi, *On the Law in General*, 28.
30. Suárez, "A Treatise on Laws," 292.

in every case. The specifics need to be supplied by a human authority, and human lawmakers have freedom in determining those details. In many situations a particular determination might take one of several forms, and because there may be no reason to prefer one form over another, the matter needs to be settled by a public authority.[31]

Road safety rules are often cited as an example. A foundational moral principle is that life should be protected; from this we can deduce, for example, that all cars should drive on the same side of the road. But the natural law does not dictate which side of the road cars should drive on; both are consistent with the moral principle. The relevant authority therefore should make a determination about this and other matters of road safety such as speed limits. A second example is whether crimes should be tried by judge alone or judge and jury. Natural law requires that justice should be done but does not specify the precise mode by which guilt should be determined. A determination needs to be made, and what is appropriate may vary from time to time.

Additions. Civil laws can also fill in detail that is not provided in the natural law. This is necessary because the moral principles contained in the natural law and the Decalogue are not sufficient of themselves for a legally enforceable rule. Translating "you shall not steal" into an enforceable legal rule requires many details to be filled in, such as defining what property is, what rights exist in property, what amounts to theft, and what penalty is to be imposed. Civil law supplies the specifics to implement the natural law in a particular context.

31. Suárez, "A Treatise on Laws," 407; Hooker, *Laws*, 1:73 [1.10.5]; Budziszewski, *Treatise on Divine Law*, 72; Budziszewski, *Companion to the Commentary*, 105.

A good example of this is the requirement of formalities for certain documents or transactions to be binding, for example, requiring witnesses to be present at a marriage or a formal written document for a valid will.[32] Imposed for good reason, such as ensuring that there was valid consent to the marriage or will, these can be considered as filling in gaps that are not covered by the natural law. Another example is the imposition of a penalty or specification of a legal consequence for the commission of an act forbidden or commanded under the natural law.

Punishments. A third important thing that civil laws do is attach earthly punishments as an inducement for people to obey.[33] For instance, people owe duties under the moral law not to steal or commit murder; civil laws make it a criminal offense to commit things such as these, attaching civil punishments such as fine or imprisonment. Theft and murder are therefore both sins under the natural law and crimes under the civil law.

One implication of these principles is that human laws are subject to change. A determination can be changed by the relevant authority.[34] The underlying moral principle is not changeable, but the particular law giving effect to it is. If it turns out that a speed limit of 40 mph would be safer than 50 mph in a particular area, the lawmaker has the freedom to change the limit. Junius argues that all positive laws have a mutable and an immutable part. The principle of the natural law that a human law gives effect to is always obligatory. However, the particular determination of a civil law only "obligates according to the persons, matters, and circumstances of those who live under them."[35] Things that follow by conclusion from general prin-

32. Suárez, "A Treatise on Laws," 303.
33. Zanchi, *On the Law in General*, 28.
34. Junius, *Mosaic Polity*, 111.
35. Junius, *Mosaic Polity*, thesis 12, 69–70, 87.

ciples should be the same everywhere; for example, we should drive carefully everywhere. But things that follow by determination of the details may vary from place to place; for example, which side of the road we must drive on.[36]

These principles helpfully chart a course between both under- and over-specificity. That is, the natural law establishes moral principles that constrain lawmakers and provide a standard against which to measure human laws. And yet natural law does not purport to give a blueprint that all lawmakers must follow in the same way; natural law allows human civil governments discretion and freedom to take into account the relevant circumstances. Natural law is not a magic formula that furnishes ready answers for every legal question that arises.[37]

It should also be noted that not all aspects of the natural law can be translated into an enforceable law by civil governments. For example, it would not be possible for a civil law to enforce the Golden Rule, or the precept that humans should seek knowledge of the truth, or that one should give generously out of one's superfluous possessions.

Civil Laws That Implement Natural Law Are Binding

One important implication follows from these principles: Civil laws that validly implement the natural law are morally obligatory.[38] Once a natural law principle is enacted into civil law through determination or addition, it is a breach of the natural law to disobey that civil law.[39] Natural law, therefore, supplies

36. Budziszewski, *Treatise on Divine Law*, 12.

37. Thomas E. Davitt, "St. Thomas Aquinas and the Natural Law," in *Origins of the Natural Law Tradition*, ed. Arthur L. Harding (Southern Methodist University Press, 1954), 45.

38. Hooker, *Laws*, 1:74 [1.10.7]; 1:77 [1.10.10].

39. Hemmingsen, *On the Law of Nature*, 162.

the requirement for obedience to human law. That is, just laws "obligate our conscience not because they come from human beings, but in part because they come from natural law to which our conscience is already obligated; and in part because God by his express command has subjected us to them."[40]

To take an example, jurisdictions typically enact road laws that make it unlawful to speed, drive through a red light, or drive while intoxicated. These things are not directly part of the natural law: There is no universally applicable rule that "you must stop at a red light." These are decisions made by a lawmaker, not inherently right or wrong in themselves. But it is a precept of the natural law that "whatever is a means of preserving human life belongs to the natural law, and whatever impedes it is contrary to it" (*ST* I-II, 94.2); or, if you prefer, "you shall not kill," which includes a broader obligation to take care not to do or permit anything that may cause injury or death to another (see Deut. 22:8). Driving while intoxicated, for example, poses an obvious risk to human life, and so is a specific instance of something that gives effect to that moral principle. As an application of the natural law, it is morally obligatory.

Suárez gives as another example the formalities relating to marriage. Marriage is part of the natural law, but natural law does not prescribe any particular formalities for a valid marriage to be concluded. Where positive law stipulates certain requirements such as witnesses, the natural law binds people to the observance of those requirements.[41]

Natural law both provides the underlying moral principle that informs the human civil law and establishes a requirement to obey any human civil laws that implement that moral principle.

40. Zanchi, *On the Law in General*, 32.
41. Suárez, "A Treatise on Laws," 320.

Civil Laws That Are Contrary to the Natural Law Are Defective

In addition to its constructive function, natural law also plays a protective function, providing a shield against laws that violate its precepts.[42] Laws that are inconsistent with the natural law are not valid laws, or at least are defective. Augustine says that "a law which is not just does not seem to me to be a law,"[43] and Aquinas says that if at any point a human law "is in any respect at odds with the law of nature, it will then no longer be law, but a corruption of law" (*ST* I-II, 95.2).

In other words, natural law asserts a necessary connection between morality (or practical reason) and law: It is of the essence of law to provide a rational set of standards to guide conduct.[44] This is often known as "the natural law thesis."

Natural law, therefore, provides an overriding standard against which to evaluate human civil laws: If a law "wanders from its source, it is degenerate, unworthy of the name of law."[45] If a human enactment attempted to impose a requirement that was not grounded in the natural law, "it would be inhumane and unreasonable, and therefore without the force of law."[46] Human law cannot override or abrogate any natural precept: "No human power can abrogate any natural precept" because natural law derives from human nature, and human law "cannot change the nature of things."[47]

42. Rice, *Fifty Questions*, 63.

43. Augustine, *De Libero Arbitrio*, trans. Dom Mark Pontifex (Longmans, Green and Co., 1955), 1.5.11.

44. Mark Murphy, "Natural Law Jurisprudence," *Legal Theory* 9 (2003): 241, 244.

45. Junius, *Mosaic Polity*, 55; Zanchi, *On the Law in General*, 27, 30–31.

46. De Vitoria, "On the American Indians," 279.

47. Suárez, "A Treatise on Laws," 309. See also Ptolemy of Lucca, *On the Government of Rulers*, 137.

How might laws be inconsistent with the natural law? Laws are unjust where they are inconsistent with the moral law, do not meet the definition of a law, attempt to regulate the conscience, are in breach of the laws of the land, exceed the authority of government, or infringe rights.[48] An improper attempt to regulate the conscience is usually understood to mean coercion in matters of belief or the attempt to force a person to act in a manner that is contrary to their beliefs. A law that permits or requires something that is contrary to the moral law, or that is for the private advantage of a lawmaker rather than the common good, or that is beyond the legitimate scope of the lawmaker's authority, is unjust.

Legal positivists reject the natural law thesis, arguing that the existence of law is a matter of social convention. On this view, law is that which is accepted as law, and there is no necessary connection between law and morality: "The existence of a law is one thing; its merits or demerits are another."[49] John Austin famously declared that "to say that a human law which conflicts with the law of God, is therefore not binding, or not valid, is to talk stark nonsense. Numberless human laws adverse to general utility, have been and are enforced in every age and nation: and yet such human laws conflict with the law of God."[50]

There is some truth to this: Lawmakers consider their decrees to be binding, even if unjust, and will enforce breaches of those decrees. In what sense, therefore, can it be said that a law that is inconsistent with the natural law is not truly a law? Different versions of the natural law thesis have been proposed. A strong version of the natural law thesis holds that a law that

48. Saunders, *The Crisis of Civil Law*, 155–65.

49. John Austin, *The Province of Jurisprudence Determined* (John Murray, 1832), 278; H. L. A. Hart, *The Concept of Law* (Clarendon Press, 1961), 181–82.

50. Austin, *Province of Jurisprudence Determined*, 279.

is inconsistent with the natural law is legally invalid; a weaker version claims that it is substandard or defective.[51]

John Finnis argues that laws that are contrary to the natural law, whether ones made in excess of authority or those that direct the doing of things that should not be done, "simply fail, of themselves, to create any moral obligation whatever." That is, there is no moral obligation to obey unjust laws.[52] Such a view, Finnis insists, does not mean that there is no sense in which unjust laws are laws. Unjust laws may be accepted as binding by the courts, and there may also be an obligation to conform to unjust laws to respect the legal system as a whole.[53]

It is not necessary to take a position on which version of the natural law thesis is correct for the purpose of this book.[54] At the least, laws that do not conform to the natural law are unjust, and there is no moral obligation to obey them. Laws that do not conform to the natural law are defective, and in cases of extreme injustice may be considered invalid. This does not mean that there is no sense in which unjust laws are laws. The question of obedience is a separate question, although obviously related.

A separate question concerns how deviations from natural law ought to be policed. In jurisdictions such as Australia, there is a strongly political model of constitutionalism whereby the merits of legislation are matters for the political branches of government (the executive and legislature). By contrast, in jurisdictions such as the United States, there is a much greater acceptance of the role of the courts in policing breaches of rights.

51. Crowe, *Natural Law and the Nature of Law*, ch. 7.

52. Finnis, *Natural Law and Natural Rights*, 360.

53. Finnis, *Natural Law and Natural Rights*, 365.

54. For a defense of the thesis, see Philip Soper, "In Defense of Classical Natural Law in Legal Theory: Why Unjust Law Is No Law at All," *Canadian Journal of Law and Jurisprudence* 20, no. 1 (2007).

Russell Hittinger has argued strongly that the question of the existence of the natural law and its relation to human positive law ought to be kept separate from the question of which institutions should have authority to make it effective within a given polity.[55] Hittinger argues against the judicialization of natural law, opining that the legislature is best placed to determine how best to particularize the natural law within a polity. Accepting the principle of natural law does not of itself entail a commitment to a strong judicial role in policing deviations from natural law (for example through the ability to strike down legislation that is not consistent with the natural law). Natural law does not prescribe the allocation of decision-making authority, and so that is something that a particular polity has freedom to determine.

Natural Law and Human Rights

Natural law, then, provides the foundation for civil government. One of the major preoccupations of civil government today is human rights. Does natural law have anything to say about rights? The relationship of natural law to human rights is a contested issue. Some have argued that "natural law" means right order and that it excludes any notion of subjective rights. For these authors, the modern notion of subjective rights is a distortion of the concept of natural law.[56] Against this, Brian Tierney argues cogently that natural law has long included concepts of subjective rights.[57]

55. Hittinger, *First Grace*, ch. 3.

56. Leo Strauss, *Natural Right and History* (University of Chicago Press, 1953); Richard Tuck, *Natural Rights Theories: Their Origin and Development* (Cambridge University Press, 1979); Virginia Black, "On Connecting Natural Rights with Natural Law," *Persona y Derecho* 22 (1990).

57. Brian Tierney, *The Idea of Natural Rights: Studies on Natural Rights, Natural Law, and Church Law, 1150–1625* (Eerdmans, 1997).

Whatever the correct interpretation of the historical material, there is a reasonable argument that natural law implies that civil governments should protect and respect the rights of people within their jurisdiction. Natural law provides an overriding and objective standard that all people are subject to, and this implies that there are limits on the powers of civil governments.

As Justice William O. Douglas of the United States Supreme Court writes, "The institutions of our society are founded on the belief that there is an authority higher than the authority of the State; that there is a moral law which the State is powerless to alter; that the individual possesses rights, conferred by the Creator, which government must respect."[58] Further, living in society with other people requires that we take their interests into account; as put by Robert George, human rights exist "if there are principles of practical reason directing us to act or abstain from acting in certain ways out of respect for the well-being and the dignity of persons whose legitimate interests may be affected by what we do."[59]

Rights under a natural law understanding would be legally enforceable claims but grounded within the concept of an objective moral order. That is, under the classical conception, rights were not accorded to people based upon a conception of personal autonomy but rather to fulfill objective goods as defined by natural and divine law.[60] A natural law approach would diverge from the modern subjective sense of rights "being absolute or presumptive barriers to governmental

58. McGowan v. Maryland, 366 U.S. 420, 562 (1960).

59. Robert P. George, "Natural Law," *American Journal of Jurisprudence* 52 (2007): 55, 57.

60. Richard H. Helmholz, "Natural Human Rights: The Perspective of the Ius Commune," *Catholic University Law Review* 52 (2003): 301.

regulation"[61] and stipulate that any rights afforded under civil law should be grounded in the natural law.[62] For example, humans are made in God's image and it is immoral to take away life; thus civil law ought to protect human life. The eighth commandment prohibits theft; this suggests the legitimacy of private property, and so civil government ought to protect property. Rights should thus be based on the objective moral order.

There are different ways in which rights may be protected by civil governments. Jurisdictions such as the United States have constitutionally enshrined rights that provide legally enforceable limits on legislative power. The Westminster model of legislative supremacy sees the protection of rights as primarily a matter for the political process, and so under this model courts do not have power to invalidate legislation that infringes rights. Hybrid models attempt to codify lists of rights but retain the supremacy of Parliament. Each of these models has its strengths and weaknesses.

Conclusion

What has been said in this chapter reflects another important claim made by classical natural law theory—that "because the moral precepts of the natural law are also the moral precepts of human reason, expressed not only within individuals but also collectively, the civil laws and legal procedures of a 'good' society will be derived from the precepts of the natural law."[63]

61. Jud Campbell, "Natural Rights and the First Amendment," *Yale Law Journal* 127 (2017): 246, 276.

62. John Witte, *God's Joust, God's Justice: Law and Religion in the Western Tradition* (Eerdmans, 2006), 31–49.

63. Pearson, "Luther's Pragmatic Appropriation," 43.

It is beyond the scope of this book to discuss the relationship between natural law and civil law in more detail.

The Protestant tradition has typically held that the law has three uses: the theological use (awakening people to a knowledge of sin), the didactic (guiding believers as to how to live to please God), and the civil or political (restraining sin and preserving peaceful and orderly society).[64] Natural law provides the foundation for the civil use of the law. The natural law tradition is concerned to show that enacting law should be guided by moral principles; "that those moral norms are a matter of objective reasonableness, not of whim, convention, or mere 'decision.'"[65] Natural law thus provides an objective and rational foundation for ethics and law.

The limitation of political power "is the very first and universally recognized preoccupation of Christian Politics."[66] And yet the teaching of Scripture is embryonic and illustrative rather than comprehensive. Natural law helps provide principles for limiting power and a standard for holding civil governments to account.

64. Bullinger, *The Decades of Henry Bullinger*, 2:237–45; Martin Chemnitz, *Loci Theologici*, trans. J. A. O. Preus (Concordia Publishing House, 1989), 800–808; Gerhard, *On the Law*, 222–25; Calvin, *Institutes of the Christian Religion*, 2.7.6–13.

65. Finnis, *Natural Law and Natural Rights*, 290.

66. Aquinas, *On Kingship*, xxxviii.

7

Some Technical Aspects of Natural Law Theory

This book has attempted to make a case that natural law is an important doctrine and is solidly based on scriptural principles and the teaching of the Christian tradition and to whet your appetite to read more. One difficulty, however, is that much of the literature on natural law is daunting and devoted to technical questions. The complexity of these issues may deter interested readers from investigating further.

This chapter therefore attempts to discuss concisely some of the issues that readers are likely to encounter when reading the literature on natural law and natural law theory. Whole volumes have been written about the issues discussed in this chapter, and I cannot do justice to those issues in a work of this nature. The purpose is not to engage in an extended technical discussion, but simply to introduce the concepts and the issues targeted at the level of a nonspecialist and to explain what (if anything) interested readers might take away from these debates.

Natural Law and the Types of Law

I have already noted that Aquinas is the most influential exponent of natural law in the history of the Christian tradition (including for many Protestant thinkers). Aquinas considered that there were four types of law—eternal, natural, human, and divine:

- Eternal law is the "rational pattern of the government of things which is in God as Ruler of the universe"—that is, the mind of God itself.
- Natural law is the participation of humans in the eternal law, which occurs by means of inclinations imprinted upon them that direct them to their proper ends and activities.
- Human laws are particular determinations of the natural law by human reason.
- Divine laws are laws specifically commanded in Scripture, which were given (among other reasons) to remove the uncertainty associated with fallible human judgment (*ST* I-II, 91.1–4).

Chapter 6 introduced the terminology of positive law. Positive laws are temporal laws, made by a particular authority at a particular time, as a determination of the natural law.[1] This does not exactly line up with the above categories. Human laws (including both civil laws and ecclesiastical laws) are instances of positive law. Many of the laws given by God in Scripture (such as the Mosaic laws) are also examples of positive laws:

1. R. H. Helmholz, "Middle Ages: Canon Law Constitutionalism?," in *Christianity and Constitutionalism*, ed. Nicholas Aroney and Ian Leigh (Oxford University Press, 2022), 121.

They are divine in origin, given for a particular purpose, and so can be described as divine positive laws.

In natural law thought, the law of nations (Latin: *ius gentium*) is the law common to civilized peoples and is broadly analogous with international law today. It was considered to include such things as the right of passage over public highways, the right to enslave introduced by war, embassage, and the hospitable treatment of foreigners and strangers.[2] This type of law occupied an ambiguous position between natural law and positive law: Many considered that the law of nations "either is or derives from natural law," while others saw it as more closely resembling human law.[3]

R. H. Helmholz argues that in classical thought, all legal systems were considered to consist of four parts: "natural law, divine law, the law of nations, and positive law." The relationship between these was as follows:

> Ideally, these four sources of law worked together in harmony, albeit at different levels of generality and with somewhat different results. The law of nature held that all men possessed a right to protect their persons and their possessions from attack, for example. The law of nations amended this slightly by assigning part of the task of protection to a system of public courts. In the interests of peace in society, all men had ceded a part of the natural law's right to the government. This being so, the civil law filled in the details of how that system functioned, establishing courts and systems of written or customary law to make the natural law's right a reality. The divine law enlarged the scope

2. Hooker, *Laws*, 1:79 [1.10.13]; Suárez, "A Treatise on Laws," 374–75.

3. De Vitoria, "On the American Indians,"278; see also xv–xvi, 281; Aquinas, *ST* I-II, 95.4; J. P. Canning, "Law, Sovereignty and Corporation Theory, 1300–1450," in *The Cambridge History of Medieval Political Thought c. 350–c. 1450*, ed. J. H. Burns (Cambridge University Press, 1988), 455.

of the resulting prohibition against theft and bodily attack to include a command not to covet the property of one's neighbors.[4]

First- and Second-Order Precepts

Writers within the Thomistic tradition argue that the natural law contains first- and second-order precepts and that some precepts of the Decalogue or natural law are deduced from other more basic principles. J. Budziszewski argues, "Just as not every moral precept in the Decalogue is purely moral, not every one of its moral precepts is general. Some, after expressing a general duty, go on to specify the particular way in which it is to be obeyed."[5] On this view, there is no inherent necessity for God to be worshiped in the manner he set out in the second commandment; it is possible that God could have determined that we worship him in a different manner. For Budziszewski, therefore, the second commandment is a determination of a moral principle.

Thomist writers also commonly argue that "do not kill" is not a primary precept of the natural law but a deduction from the more fundamental precept that we should do no harm to others.[6] Similarly, the commandment "do not commit adultery" is considered to be a deduction from the broader principle of the union of male and female. Thus, Thomist writers distinguish between those things that are considered to be self-evident and those that must be deduced from the primary principles.[7]

This approach, in my view, introduces an unnecessary level of artificiality and may also be inconsistent with the fact that the biblical commands are consistent with God's nature. It is true

4. Helmholz, "Middle Ages," 121.
5. Budziszewski, *Treatise on Divine Law*, 165.
6. Aquinas, *ST* I-II, 95.2; Rice, *Fifty Questions*, 62.
7. See, e.g., Aquinas, *ST* I-II, 100.3; Suárez, "A Treatise on Laws," 235.

that the moral law can be summarized in more fundamental or basic ways. As is often noted, the Decalogue is typically considered to be a perfect summary of the moral law, and the Decalogue itself can be summarized in the two great commandments, love for God and love for neighbor.[8] The two great commandments, or alternatively the commands of the Decalogue itself, could be considered to be the primary precepts of the moral law.

The commandment "you shall not kill" could be seen not as a deduction from another supposedly more fundamental principle but as itself a primary precept of the natural law, evident from the creation of humans in God's image. Indeed, there is no biblical warrant for treating "do no harm to others" as a more primary and fundamental precept from which "you shall not kill" is derived.

The underlying rationale of the second commandment is that it is impossible to represent God visually, and so it may be simply incorrect that God could have determined that we worship Him in a different manner. In any case, there is no more fundamental moral principle regarding the worship of God that exists apart from and prior to the specific determination given in the second commandment.

Metaphysics and Natural Law

There is much debate in natural law literature around the metaphysical underpinnings of natural law. There is a cluster of related questions here. Does the existence of natural law depend on the existence of God? Does the principle of natural law depend on metaphysical foundations about human nature? Does our knowledge of natural law depend on knowledge of those metaphysical foundations? Different positions

8. Matt. 22:36–40; Deut. 6:4–9; Lev. 19:18.

have been advocated on these issues, and I will lay them out briefly below.

Does the existence of natural law depend on the existence of God? It may seem surprising that there is a debate within the natural law tradition as to whether natural law depends on the existence of God. The classical conception of natural law clearly grounds natural law within a reality that was created and ordered by God. Aquinas, as we have seen, expressly embeds natural law within a concept of eternal law, which is nothing less than divine reason. For Aquinas, natural law is human participation in the eternal law.[9] Brian McCall argues that "classical natural law jurisprudence is intellectually unsustainable without teleology, and teleology requires a being that is above teleological reality."[10]

By contrast, writers such as John Finnis have sought to develop theories of natural law that significantly downplay its grounding in God. Finnis has articulated a detailed account of natural law, which explains the goods that humans should pursue and the nature of practical reasonableness, with minimal reference to the existence or nature of God. It is not that Finnis does not believe in God; he adopts this approach in order to articulate an account of natural law that is comprehensible to modern secular readers.[11] According to Finnis, therefore, it is possible to articulate a detailed account of natural law with minimal reference to God.

Does natural law depend on metaphysical truths about human nature? Both Roman Catholic and Protestant writers argue that

9. In similar vein, Oliver O'Donovan considers that "morality is man's participation in the created order": *Resurrection and Moral Order*, 76.

10. Brian M. McCall, *The Architecture of Law: Rebuilding Law in the Classical Tradition* (University of Notre Dame Press, 2018), 422. See, to similar effect, Walker, *Faithful Reason*, 29, 87, 147–49.

11. Finnis writes, "Reading my way into the natural law tradition, as a final-year law student and then during my doctoral studies, I was disconcerted by the inability or unwillingness of the modern writers in that tradition to meet modern secular students as and where they are." *Natural Law and Natural Rights*, 415.

natural law depends on metaphysical foundations—namely, truths about reality and human nature. According to Heinrich Rommen, throughout history natural law has only obtained general acceptance when there is widespread commitment to metaphysics. Thus, natural law depends on metaphysics—namely, the science of being.[12] Many insist that these foundations must be understood in Aristotelian or Thomist terms. David Haines and Andrew Fulford argue that "a consistent Christian natural law theory" must be built upon the philosophical foundations of Aristotelian metaphysics.[13] Some scholars articulate this at a high level of detail and complexity.[14]

Does our knowledge of natural law depend on knowledge of those metaphysical foundations? As just noted, it is widely accepted that the existence and content of natural law depend on truths about human nature. A closely related question is whether our knowledge of natural law depends on knowledge of those metaphysical foundations. Writers in the Thomist tradition often argue that knowledge of the precepts of the natural law is arrived at through speculative reflection on human nature—that is, that metaphysical knowledge of human nature precedes knowledge of ethical norms.[15] Simply perceiving the existence of human inclinations is not enough; only by appreciating how those inclinations are consistent with the rational order and human nature can they be perceived as good or morally obliging.[16]

12. Heinrich A. Rommen, *The Natural Law: A Study in Legal and Social History and Philosophy*, trans. Thomas R. Hanley (Liberty Fund, 1998), 141.

13. Haines and Fulford, *Natural Law*, 2–3.

14. E.g., Lisska, *Aquinas's Theory of Natural Law*, 85.

15. R. J. Matava, "On Knowing the Natural Law: A Response to Steven Jensen," *American Journal of Jurisprudence* 61, no. 2 (2016): 237, 239; Robert P. George, "Natural Law and Human Nature," in *Natural Law Theory: Contemporary Essays*, ed. Robert P. George (Clarendon Press, 1992), 32.

16. Oderberg, "The Metaphysical Foundations of Natural Law," 70–74; William C. Mattison III, "The Changing Face of Natural Law: The Necessity of

Brian McCall argues that "speculative reason is necessary to understand the basic truths on which the existence and obligatory nature of natural law rest: the end and nature of man. Practical reason is necessary to reach conclusions oriented toward actions based on these truths."[17] According to the classical account of natural law, "all human duties and human rights may be reasonably adjudged to be duties and rights only insofar as they can be justified, and thus shown to be duties or rights, in the light of man's natural end and perfection."[18]

By contrast, others argue that our knowledge of natural law is not dependent on knowledge of the metaphysical foundations. The "new natural law" school of Germain Grisez and John Finnis argues that the basic forms of good are self-evident and are not derived or inferred from metaphysical or teleological conceptions of human nature.[19] As put by Jonathan Crowe, "the basic goods, according to Grisez and Finnis, are self-evident and underived. They are not the result of speculative inquiry into the natural properties of humans or anything else. Rather, they are grasped noninferentially by anyone engaging in practical choice."[20]

The controversy here is not about the nature of reality, but how we know that reality. Both the classical and new natural law approaches agree that natural law depends on human nature. Finnis notes that metaphysically or ontologically, it is true that the content of natural law depends on human nature.[21] However, he considers that our awareness of the content of

Belief for Natural Law Norm Specification," *Journal of the Society of Christian Ethics* 27, no. 1 (2007): 251, 265–66.

17. McCall, *The Architecture of Law*, 178.

18. Henry B. Veatch, "Natural Law: Dead or Alive?," in Henry B. Veatch, *Swimming Against the Current in Contemporary Philosophy* (Catholic University of America Press, 1990), 265.

19. Finnis, *Natural Law and Natural Rights*, 33–34, 371.

20. Crowe, *Natural Law and the Nature of Law*, 23.

21. Finnis, *Natural Law and Natural Rights*, 416.

natural law does not depend on awareness of human nature.[22] Thus, Finnis argues that practical knowledge is not deduced or inferred from speculative facts about human nature. Instead, we acquire knowledge of the goods and from there determine facts about human nature.[23]

It is important to draw a distinction between the metaphysical (i.e., the nature of reality) and the epistemological (i.e., our knowledge of the nature of reality) aspects of natural law. That is, we need to separate the two questions:

- The ontological or metaphysical question: Does natural law depend on metaphysical foundations about human nature?
- The epistemological question: Does our knowledge of natural law depend on knowledge of those metaphysical foundations?

As noted, there is widespread agreement about the answer to the first question. The dispute, then, is a relatively narrow one, relating to whether we derive knowledge of the good from knowledge of human nature or vice versa. The literature on these issues is complex, and I cannot do it justice here.[24]

The approach I take in this book is that natural law depends on metaphysical truths about human nature but that it is not necessary to know those truths in order to grasp many aspects of the natural law. Similarly, natural law depends on

22. Jensen, *Knowing the Natural Law*, 18.

23. John Finnis, "Aquinas and Natural Law Jurisprudence," in *The Cambridge Companion to Natural Law Jurisprudence*, ed. George Duke and Robert P. George (Cambridge University Press, 2017), 19, 34–35. See also Walker, *Faithful Reason*, 144–46.

24. See, e.g., Jensen, *Knowing the Natural Law*; Finnis, *Natural Law and Natural Rights*; McCall, *The Architecture of Law*.

the existence of God, but it is not necessary to believe in God in order to grasp many aspects of the natural law.

Metaphysically, natural law depends on the existence of God and truths about human nature. In order to develop a fully satisfying and complete account of natural law, it needs to be grounded on those foundations. However, epistemologically, it is not necessary to know metaphysical facts about human nature in order to understand and grasp precepts of the natural law.

The truths of natural law can be grasped without understanding those metaphysical truths about human nature, and without believing in God. Many people grasp moral truth without believing in God or accepting a Christian understanding of humankind.[25]

As I noted in chapter 5, natural law thinkers often argue that it is impossible not to know the foundational precepts of the natural law. To take an example, all people recognize that it is wrong to kill the innocent. But many people do not recognize or accept the underlying metaphysical basis for this—namely, that humans are made in God's image. They are nevertheless able to perceive the truth that murder is wrong. The scriptural teaching, as discussed in chapter 2, is consistent with this view.

Do we perceive the good and then determine truths about human nature or does knowledge of human nature necessarily precede knowledge of the good? I doubt that there is one single means of acquiring knowledge of the moral law that can be generalized for all people. In any case it is not necessary to take a position on this debate for the purposes of this book.

It is also worthwhile recalling the distinction between natural law and natural law theory from chapter 1. As noted there,

25. Patrick Lee, "God and New Natural Law Theory," *The National Catholic Bioethics Quarterly* 19, no. 2 (2019): 280, 287.

people can discern moral truth outside of Scripture and so can perceive moral truth (imperfectly) without believing in God. It is possible to know the truths of the natural law without God or without understanding underlying metaphysical truths about humankind. However, it is not possible to develop a satisfying and complete theory of natural law without God or metaphysical truths about human nature.

The Metaphysical Underpinnings of Natural Law

The previous section argued that natural law depends on metaphysical truths about human nature (and there is widespread agreement within the natural law tradition about this) but that it is not necessary to know those truths in order to grasp many aspects of the natural law. What, then, are the metaphysical underpinnings of natural law? A detailed discussion of metaphysics in natural law theory is beyond the scope of this book.

David S. Oderberg argues that natural law relies upon essentialism—namely, that all things have their own essence and that these essences "are real and knowable."[26] A similar argument is made by Haines and Fulford, who ground natural law upon moderate realism, the view that created essences exist and that essences can be known.[27]

In natural law literature, human nature is often articulated in Aristotelian and Thomist categories. Aristotle famously argued that there were four causes or explanations for any why-question:

- the material cause: that from which a thing comes into being, such as the bronze of a statue;

26. Oderberg, "The Metaphysical Foundations of Natural Law," 60.
27. Haines and Fulford, *Natural Law*, 23.

- the formal cause: the form or pattern, such as the shape of the statue;
- the efficient cause: that which brings about the change, such as the artisan who sculpts the statue; and
- the final cause: the end, "that for the sake of which a thing is," such as health being the purpose of walking.[28]

These categories, especially the telos or final cause, are often used in Thomist writing to define the essence of a thing, and what makes something right or wrong. For instance, Aquinas's argument that humans have a natural inclination to ends that include self-preservation, reproduction, knowing the truth concerning God, and living in society is clearly based on teleological categories (*ST* I-II, 94.2). For Aquinas, the final cause is that which determines the development or perfection of a human inclination and indeed describes human nature or essence.[29]

There are several comments we can make about this. First, metaphysical propositions about human nature are fallible. Natural law is the principle that there is a moral order and that this moral order is based in the nature of reality. Thomist-Aristotelian metaphysics is one possible way of describing the nature of reality. These categories are not infallible, and they are not the only possible way of accurately describing reality. James Jordan's comments are applicable here: "In the Western world for several centuries, men have assumed that the proper way to express truth is by means of abstract, philosophical language. Wherever we find imagery, parable, symbolism, or

28. Aristotle, *Metaphysics*, in *The Complete Works of Aristotle: The Revised Oxford Translation*, ed. Jonathan Barnes (Princeton University Press, 1984), V.2.
29. Lisska, *Aquinas's Theory of Natural Law*, 87, 183–84.

typology, we ought to translate such language into proper abstractions. This, however, is not how God chose to reveal Himself to us."[30]

There may be value in translating the concrete depictions of reality that appear in Scripture into the abstract formulations of Aristotelianism and scholastic theology. However, it is not necessary to do so to hold to natural law. That is, it is not necessary to accept philosophical categories such as those held by Aquinas or Aristotle in order to accept the principle of natural law.

Intellectualism and Voluntarism

One issue that has absorbed a great deal of scholarly attention is whether natural law should be understood in intellectualist terms, as primarily an act of God's reason, or alternatively in voluntarist terms, as primarily an act of his will. The intellectualist, or realist, view considers the natural law to be "an intellectual act independent of Will . . . as the dictate of Reason as to what is right, grounded in the Being of God but unalterable even by him." By contrast, the voluntarist position considers the natural law to consist of divine commands, binding simply because they are commanded by God.[31]

An intellectualist view may seem to diminish God's freedom to act, while a voluntarist approach seems to make morality purely arbitrary: If what is good is simply what is commanded, then God is able to grant dispensations from or even change the natural law.[32] A view that sees law as solely dependent on the

30. James B. Jordan, *Through New Eyes: Developing a Biblical View of the World* (Wolgemuth & Hyatt, 1988), 30.

31. Otto von Gierke, *Political Theories of the Middle Ages*, trans. F. W. Maitland (Cambridge University Press, 1922), 172–73.

32. See, e.g., Suárez, "A Treatise on Laws," 326–55.

divine will has obvious parallels with legal positivism, which Christians ought to resist.

It is often argued that Aquinas considered God's intellect to be logically prior to his will, and so he is firmly within the intellectualist camp.[33] It is also commonly argued that the voluntarist position influenced leading Reformation thinkers such as Luther and Calvin, and so voluntarism is characteristic of Protestant theology.[34] For instance, Calvin writes that "God's will is so much the highest rule of righteousness that whatever he wills, by the very fact that he wills it, must be considered righteous" and that no higher reason can be given for God's actions.[35]

It was a widely held view within the field of biblical scholarship for many years that the redemption of Israel was central to the Old Testament and that an appeal to a moral order inherent in the world was the antithesis of the biblical teaching on ethics.[36] Influential scholars such as Gerhard von Rad viewed the doctrine of creation as secondary to the message of salvation, and so biblical scholars tended to emphasize the idea that ethics derive solely from God's revealed commands.[37]

This is a question with a long and complex history. For the purposes of this book, I suggest that two principles provide a helpful way of thinking through the issue. The first relates to the definition of *law*. As noted earlier, Aquinas defines *law* as an "ordinance of reason for the common good, made and promulgated by him who has care of the community" (*ST* I-II, 90.4). While

33. E.g., Kai Nielsen, "An Examination of the Thomistic Theory of Natural Moral Law," *Natural Law Forum* 4, no. 1 (1959), 44, 50; Lisska, *Aquinas's Theory of Natural Law*, 89.

34. W. J. Torrance Kirby, *Richard Hooker, Reformer and Platonist* (Taylor & Francis, 2016), 63.

35. Calvin, *Institutes of the Christian Religion*, 3.23.2.

36. Barton, *Ethics in Ancient Israel*, 94.

37. Haas, "Creational Ethics Is Public Ethics," 5.

this seems to place reason at the core of the definition of *law*, and might be thought to support an intellectualist account, it also recognizes that any law needs to be "made and promulgated."

This means that there must be an act of will that gives effect to and implements a dictate of reason in order for a law to come into existence: "The fact there is a command requires an act of will, but what the command directs requires an act of reason." Thus, reason and will function together: "The function of reason is to identify the purpose that is to be pursued, which is always some good, and to work out what must be done to achieve it. . . . The function of will, in turn, is to command what reason has indicated."[38]

Even though Aquinas is often associated with an intellectualist account, his view of God's freedom also cautions against downplaying God's will. He writes,

> God does not act from natural necessity, but [. . .] His will is the cause of all things; nor is that will naturally and from any necessity determined to those things. Whence in no way at all is the present course of events produced by God from any necessity, so that other things could not happen . . . the divine wisdom is not so restricted to any particular order that no other course of events could happen. Wherefore we must simply say that God can do other things than those He has done. (*ST* I, 25.5)

Second, the doctrine of the simplicity of God posits that God's essence is identical with his existence and "asserts the essential identity of God with all of his attributes or qualities."[39] That is, God's attributes "are not severable from who God is"; they

38. Budziszewski, *Treatise on Law*, 18, 26.

39. Richard A. Muller, *Post-Reformation Reformed Dogmatics: The Rise and Development of Reformed Orthodoxy, ca. 1520 to ca. 1725*, 2nd ed. (Baker Academic, 2003), 3:43–44, 53; Aquinas, *ST* I, 3.4.

are "not descriptions of what sort of being God is" but "statements of 'what' God is."[40] If so, God's will cannot be conceived as something separate from his wisdom: "Divine will is not separate from divine wisdom."[41]

As put by J. Budziszewski, to put God's reason above his will is to introduce an artificial separation: "Certainly St. Thomas doesn't put God's will above His reason, but neither does he put His reason above His will . . . in Him, will and reason are not distinct from each other. They are the same Divine Essence, viewed in two different ways."[42] The divine will does not act separately from the divine reason.[43]

Conclusion

This chapter has briefly examined some of the key technical issues relating to natural law that readers are likely to encounter in the natural law literature. Although this discussion cannot do justice to those issues, I have endeavored to suggest what Protestant readers ought to make of them. Notwithstanding that people may disagree about these issues, this does not disturb the fact that there is a core set of principles relating to natural law that all Christians ought to be able to accept.

40. Benjamin B. Saunders, "The Loving Sword: The Implications of Divine Simplicity for Law and Love," in *Christianity, Ethics and the Law: The Concept of Love in Christian Legal Thought*, ed. Zachary R. Calo, Joshua Neoh, and A. Keith Thompson (Routledge, 2023), 116.

41. Zanchi, *On the Law in General*, 14.

42. Budziszewski, *Treatise on Law*, 199.

43. Charles E. Rice, "Some Reasons for a Restoration of Natural Law Jurisprudence," *Wake Forest Law Review* 24 (1989): 565–66.

8

Common Questions and Objections

There have been many objections to the idea of natural law throughout history, from within and outside the Christian tradition. As this book has progressed, I have been addressing various questions about and objections to natural law that Protestants typically have. Here, I want to look at a few further common objections, including some that have often been made by non-Christians. Many of the objections made by non-Christians will not be persuasive to Christians, such as the commonly held view that morality is relative. Likewise, another common objection to natural law, the naturalistic fallacy, is not compatible with scriptural teaching.

I start this chapter by discussing these two objections to natural law commonly made by non-Christians, but I focus mainly on the objections made in Protestant circles.

The Naturalistic Fallacy

Perhaps the most common objection to natural law is the naturalistic fallacy. This argument is often traced back to David

Hume, who famously argued that "ought" and "ought not" statements were entirely different from "is" and "is not" statements and needed to be defended in their own right.[1] It is commonly argued that natural law improperly seeks to derive ought statements from observations about, for example, human nature, thereby committing the naturalistic fallacy.[2]

World-renowned ethicist Peter Singer provides an excellent example of an argument that falls into the naturalistic fallacy: "Whales cannot be humanely killed: they are too large—even with explosive harpoons it is difficult to hit the right spot. And because whalers are reluctant to use large amounts of explosive, which would destroy valuable oil or flesh, harpooned whales typically die slowly and painfully. If there were some life-and-death need that humans could meet only by killing whales, perhaps the ethical case could be countered. But everything we get from whales can be obtained without cruelty elsewhere. Thus, whaling is unethical."[3]

Evidently enough, the conclusion "whaling is unethical" does not follow from the premise "everything we get from whales can be obtained without cruelty elsewhere." Another premise is needed, something like "If it is possible to obtain X without inflicting cruelty or physical pain on an animal, then it is unethical to obtain X by inflicting cruelty on an animal."

It may be conceded that there is a sense in which the naturalistic fallacy is correct. It is true that, in sound logical reasoning, a conclusion cannot contain anything that is not already present in the premises.[4] As such, "no value can be deduced or other-

1. David Hume, *A Treatise of Human Nature* (Penguin, 1985), 521 [3.1.1].

2. Nielsen, "Examination of the Thomistic Theory," 44, 59.

3. Peter Singer, "Harpooned by Hypocrisy," *The Guardian*, January 20, 2008, https://www.theguardian.com/commentisfree/2008/jan/19/animalwelfare.uk.

4. Jensen, *Knowing the Natural Law*, 2.

wise inferred from a fact or set of facts."[5] The mere fact that, for example, most people get married and have children does not mean that people ought to do this, or that this is good: It may be that this is simply what happens.

However, the naturalistic fallacy is not something that the Bible accepts as valid.[6] The creation is not simply bare existence, free from objective value: Scripture teaches that the world is the handiwork of an all-good, all-powerful Creator, who pronounced all things "very good" (Gen. 1:31). I have argued in this book that the world is not neutral but has been made according to God's good, wise, and loving design, is subject to a moral order, and is invested with "normative moral significance."[7]

From this order, certain moral consequences follow. As noted earlier, in Mark 10 Jesus quotes from Genesis 2:23–24 to draw conclusions about the inviolability of marriage. The logic here is that because God has made the world in a certain way ("from the beginning of creation, 'God made them male and female'" [Mark 10:6]), therefore moral consequences follow ("what therefore God has joined together, let not man separate" [v. 9]). That is, Jesus here draws an "ought" from an "is." That is only possible because marriage and the complementarity of male and female are part of God's good creation. Another example is the fourth commandment: God made the world in six days and rested on the seventh, establishing a pattern that people ought to follow (Exod. 20:8–11).

These two texts tell us that the creation narrative in Genesis is not the mere recording of events or facts that have no ongoing

5. Finnis, *Natural Law and Natural Rights*, 66.

6. For further criticism, see Oderberg, *Moral Theory*, 11–15.

7. Bernd Wannenwetsch, "Creation and Ethics: On the Legitimacy and Limitation of Appeals to 'Nature' in Christian Moral Reasoning," in *Within the Love of God: Essays on the Doctrine of God in Honour of Paul S. Fiddes*, ed. Anthony Clarke and Andrew Moore (Oxford University Press, 2014), 209.

significance. Rather, it sets out patterns and norms that remain normative. Because "God made them male and female," certain moral implications and consequences follow, including the proper pattern for sex and marital union, reproduction, and the inviolability of marriage. Similarly, the law expressly connects the weekly Sabbath with the pattern established in creation. The world is not morally neutral in the way envisaged by many modern philosophers.

A second point is worth reiterating. At first blush, the principles of natural law as articulated by Aquinas and others may appear to be inferences drawn from observed facts. However, this is not the case. The precept (for example) of self-preservation is not an inference drawn from observation, but it is a prescriptive and normatively binding principle of practical reason that we recognize as self-evidently true. Human life is a good thing that ought to be preserved. Thus, the principles of natural law are not "is" statements but have oughtness built into them.

Morality Is Relative

Another common non-Christian objection to the idea of natural law is that there is no such thing as objective morality and no such thing as a universal human nature. The primary virtue today is tolerance, and people profess not to believe in "discoverable and objectively valid" moral principles.[8] There are different versions of such a view. For example, some argue that there are no such things as objective moral truths and that moral

8. John Hart Ely, *Democracy and Distrust: A Theory of Judicial Review* (University Press, 1980), 54; Allan Bloom, *The Closing of the American Mind: How Higher Education Has Failed Democracy and Impoverished the Souls of Today's Students* (Simon & Schuster, 1987).

statements are simply statements of opinion. Others argue that no moral standpoint is uniquely privileged over others and that the correctness of beliefs about what is right and wrong is dependent on given frameworks, such as local cultural norms or individual standards.[9]

In an influential article, judge Richard A. Posner argues:

> There are no *interesting* moral universals. There are tautological ones, such as "Murder is wrong," where "murder" means "wrongful killing," and there are a few rudimentary principles of social cooperation—such as "Don't lie all the time" or "Don't break promises without any reason" or "Don't kill your relatives or neighbors indiscriminately"—that may be common to all human societies. If one wants to call these rudimentary principles the universal moral law, fine; but as a practical matter, no moral code can be criticized by appealing to norms that are valid across cultures, norms to which the code of a particular culture is a better or a worse approximation. Those norms, the rudimentary principles of social cooperation that I have mentioned, are too abstract to serve as standards for moral judgment. Any meaningful moral realism is therefore out, and moral relativism . . . is in.[10]

Two responses can be made to this. First, many profess that morality is relative or subjective, but in fact our generation has many moral absolutes, such as the following:

- Do not be racist.
- Do not discriminate against anyone based on sex, sexual preference, gender, or race.

9. "Relativism," Stanford Encyclopedia of Philosophy, updated January 10, 2025, https://plato.stanford.edu/entries/relativism; "Relativism," Internet Encyclopedia of Philosophy, https://iep.utm.edu/relativi.

10. Richard A. Posner, "The Problematics of Moral and Legal Theory," *Harvard Law Review* 111 (1997): 1637, 1640.

- Do not engage in sexual activity without consent.
- Do not abuse children.
- Men: Do not oppress women.
- You must affirm every person's sexual preferences.
- You must affirm every person's chosen gender identity.

A relativist would no doubt retort that these happen to be the moral preferences that currently prevail in modern Western democracies. Nevertheless, the fact that our society believes these things to be right, and that other less enlightened countries should adopt these beliefs, illustrates that it is patently incorrect that we believe morality is merely subjective or relative.[11]

Second, this is obviously not a valid objection from a Christian perspective, which recognizes that there is a universally applicable moral law deriving from the law of the Creator. We all believe in moral "laws." The question is, Where do these moral truths come from—who decides their content? One key purpose of a natural law doctrine is to provide an objective standard for morality.

There Are Too Many Inconsistent Views of Natural Law

This objection, expressed by some Christians, claims that natural law has been used throughout history to justify a wide range of inconsistent positions. Aristotle notoriously argued that some men were slaves by nature and so slavery was sanctioned

11. Posner himself is reported to have said in 2014 that preventing gay marriage derives from "a tradition of hate . . . and savage discrimination": "Judges Chide State Lawyers over Gay Marriage Bans," *Associated Press*, August 27, 2014, https://apnews.com/4b086ba410884595b6b2549a06747756.

by the natural law.[12] Grotius similarly argued that slavery was legitimate in certain circumstances, extending Aristotle's view to entire nations: "As Aristotle said, some Men are naturally Slaves, that is, turned for Slavery. And some Nations also are of such a Temper, that they know better how to obey than to command."[13]

Theologians such as Francisco de Vitoria argue based on natural law that "barbarians" such as the American Indians possessed rightful ownership of their property and therefore that they could not rightfully be despoiled of their property.[14] Hugo Grotius holds the opposite, arguing that "war is lawful against those who offend against Nature" based on a power of punishment that proceeds from natural law.[15]

The belief that certain races or ethnic groups are inferior has been based on natural law and appeals to nature.[16] Natural law plays a key role in a recent argument for Christian nationalism.[17] Natural law has been used to justify the denial of rights to women such as the right to vote or to attend a university.[18] In 1873, Justice Joseph P. Bradley of the United States Supreme Court wrote:

> The civil law, as well as nature herself, has always recognized a wide difference in the respective spheres and destinies of man and woman. . . . The natural and proper timidity and delicacy which belongs to the female sex evidently unfits it for many

12. Aristotle, *Politics*, 1.5, 1254b16–39.

13. Grotius, *The Rights of War and Peace*, 1:264 [I.III.8]; 2:557 [II.V.27], 2:559–61 [II.V.29]; 1:xxx–xxxi.

14. De Vitoria, "On the American Indians."

15. Grotius, *The Rights of War and Peace*, 2:1024 [II.XX.40].

16. Allen Mendenhall, *The Three Ps of Liberty: Pragmatism, Pluralism, and Polycentricity* (Palgrave Macmillan, 2020), ch. 3.

17. Stephen Wolfe, *The Case for Christian Nationalism* (Canon Press, 2022).

18. Favale, *Genesis of Gender*, 147.

> of the occupations of civil life. The constitution of the family organization, which is founded in the divine ordinance as well as in the nature of things, indicates the domestic sphere as that which properly belongs to the domain and functions of womanhood. . . . The paramount destiny and mission of woman are to fulfill the noble and benign offices of wife and mother. This is the law of the Creator.[19]

More recently, there have been attempts to argue that there is a natural right to assisted suicide.[20] Some judges have even suggested that people have a natural law right of abortion on the basis that there is an inherent right to privacy that warrants the exclusion of governmental interference in relation to such decisions.[21]

Natural law has thus been subject to a wide array of conflicting claims.[22] This would seem to cast doubt on the existence of a universally applicable moral order, knowable through human reason. What are we to make of this? Do those who believe in natural law have a "naive state of mind" that considers that what is familiar to them must be accepted by all people everywhere?[23]

First, there is substantial agreement on core aspects of the natural law.[24] Arguments about the range of conflicting views of the content of natural law may overstate the extent of disagreement.

Second, the history of the church is littered with controversy about practically every theological doctrine, even those that are

19. Bradwell v. State of Illinois, 83 U.S. 130, 141 (1873).

20. Hittinger, *First Grace*, ch. 6.

21. See Planned Parenthood South Atlantic v. State of South Carolina (2022), South Carolina Supreme Court, January 5, 2023, https://www.sccourts.org/opinions/HTMLFiles/SC/28127.pdf.

22. James Luther Adams, "The Law of Nature: Some General Considerations," *Journal of Religion* 25, no. 2 (1945): 88–96.

23. Oliver Wendell Holmes, "Natural Law," *Harvard Law Review* 32, no. 1 (1918): 40, 41.

24. See Adams, "Law of Nature," 95.

seemingly very clearly spelled out in Scripture. In this way, natural law is no different from most other doctrines. The existence of disagreement does not prove natural law wrong; it merely proves that humans have an infinite capacity for distorting the truth (see Rom. 3:4).

Third, it is worthwhile recalling the distinction between natural law and natural law theory: Natural law is the objective reality of the moral order, while natural law theory is what humans have thought about the natural law.[25] The fact that there has been disagreement within natural law theory does not entail that there is no objective moral order. Scripture itself teaches the existence of a moral order that is knowable through the conscience and provides an authoritative statement of the moral law.

In chapter 3, I suggested that there are some extrabiblical precepts that ought to be considered morally binding. However, we ought to be cautious before laying down moral prescriptions that are not clearly taught in the Bible. Some aspects of natural law are clear and incontrovertible (for example, that murder is wrong). Others are less so (for example, whether contraception is right or wrong). This lack of complete certainty is not fatal to the idea of natural law but rather serves to recognize its limitations. The point of natural law is not to provide a simplistic means of achieving certainty on every conceivable question.

Natural Law Is Either Too Particular to Be Universal or Too Vague to Be Useful

Another objection leveled at natural law is that it is trapped on the horns of a dilemma. As put by Roberto Unger, "All the

25. VanDrunen, "Should Protestants Reject Natural Law? Responding to Common Objections," *Public Discourse*, August 2, 2020, https://www.thepublicdiscourse.com/2020/08/67076.

many attempts to build a moral and political doctrine upon the conception of a universal human nature have failed. They are repeatedly trapped in a dilemma. Either the allegedly universal ends are too few and abstract to give content to the idea of the good, or they are too numerous and concrete to be truly universal. One has to choose between triviality and implausibility."[26] A similar point is made by Jean Porter, who argues that Aquinas's concept of natural law cannot be made to yield "normative precepts that are both specific enough to be put into practice and valid and binding in all times and places."[27]

However, this is a false dilemma. Or, to put it another way, it is as much a strength of natural law as a weakness. I have argued above that, despite the diversity of human cultures, there are in fact universal features of human nature. As argued by John Finnis, there seems to be a "universality of a few basic values in a vast diversity of realizations," including widespread respect for goods such as life, procreation, and friendship.[28] As explored in chapter 2, the Bible clearly recognizes that there are universally applicable moral norms and universal features of human nature.

The supposed dilemma rests on a misunderstanding of the principle of natural law.[29] There is indeed an attraction in an approach that offers the false hope of making prudential decisions easy.[30] But natural law does not purport to provide a

26. Roberto Mangabeira Unger, *Knowledge and Politics* (Free Press, 1975).

27. Jean Porter, "Does the Natural Law Provide a Universally Valid Morality?," in *Intractable Disputes About the Natural Law: Alasdair MacIntyre and Critics*, ed. Lawrence Cunningham (University of Notre Dame Press, 2009), 55. See also Thielicke, *Theological Ethics*, 1:393; Posner, "Problematics of Moral and Legal Theory," 1637, 1640–41, 1650.

28. Finnis, *Natural Law and Natural Rights*, 83–84.

29. A misunderstanding of this nature seems to underlie Helmut Thielicke's concerns with natural law: Thielicke, *Theological Ethics*, 1:388–94.

30. Budziszewski, *Companion to the Commentary*, 183.

catalog of neat a priori answers to all questions. The moral law is indeterminate, and it is up to humans to particularize it in different contexts. If we expect natural law to resolve all contested questions of public policy, we are mistaken.[31] There are of course black-and-white rules such as "do not murder." But natural law is better thought of as a reasonable guide to principles rather than a cookbook of legal recipes.[32]

As discussed in chapter 5, the nature of practical reason is to deliberate about action, and this involves the application of general principles to particular circumstances, and circumstances vary widely. Variation in the application of the principles of natural law is not a defect of natural law; it is an inevitable result of varying circumstances.

Let us now consider some specifically Protestant objections to the doctrine of natural law.

The Sufficiency of Scripture

One common Protestant concern is that natural law undermines the principle of the sufficiency of Scripture. It is sometimes thought that, by positing the existence of extrabiblical moral norms, natural law undermines the priority of Scripture and is inconsistent with the principle of *sola scriptura*. It is worthwhile comparing and contrasting how Scripture is treated under the Protestant and Roman Catholic accounts of natural law.

Roman Catholic teaching is, needless to say, inconsistent with this principle. The papal encyclical *Humanae Vitae* states that Christ constituted the Roman magisterium "as the authentic

31. Cf. Ely, *Democracy and Distrust*, 52.
32. Rice, *Fifty Questions*, 63.

guardians and interpreters of the whole moral law, not only, that is, of the law of the Gospel but also of the natural law. For the natural law, too, declares the will of God, and its faithful observance is necessary for men's eternal salvation."[33] The church further affirms that "the faithful are obliged to acknowledge and respect the specific moral precepts declared and taught by the Church in the name of God, the Creator and Lord."[34]

The *Catechism of the Catholic Church* states that "to the Church belongs the right always and everywhere to announce moral principles" and "the authority of the Magisterium extends also to the specific precepts of the natural law, because their observance, demanded by the Creator, is necessary for salvation."[35] Thus, the Roman Catholic Church considers itself to be the authoritative interpreter of natural law and maintains that, in order to be saved, it is necessary to adhere to the Roman Catholic Church's pronouncements on natural law.

A genuinely Protestant account of natural law will, of course, have a different approach to authority. The *Westminster Confession of Faith* states, "God alone is Lord of the conscience, and has left it free from the doctrines and commandments of men, which are, in any thing, contrary to His Word; or beside it, in matters of faith, or worship. So that, to believe such doctrines, or to obey such commands, out of conscience, is to betray true liberty of conscience: and the requiring of an implicit faith, and an absolute and blind obedience, is to destroy liberty of conscience, and reason also" (*WCF* 20.2).

Protestant theology holds that Scripture is the final and only inspired authority and rejects the pretensions of Rome. This does not deny the relevance of other sources of knowledge.

33. Pope Paul VI, *Humanae Vitae*, 4.
34. John Paul II, *Veritatis Splendor* (August 6, 1993), 76.
35. *Catechism of the Catholic Church*, 491–92 [2032–36].

The principle of *sola scriptura* is that "only Scripture, because it is God's inspired Word, is our inerrant, sufficient, and final authority for the church" and rejects tradition as a source of divine revelation.[36]

This does not mean that extrabiblical data is irrelevant, including in relation to the principles of morality. The Bible does not provide all information on every conceivable subject. The principle of *sola scriptura* is not that "Scripture is the only authority or the only source from which we can draw," but that it alone is the "supreme and final authority in all of life and therefore sufficient." Other sources are useful and valuable, but always to be recognized as fallible and subordinate to the Bible.[37] Any "serious evangelical Christian ethic" must recognize that "there are two chief sources of ethical knowledge" that must be held together. While Scripture is always the final authority, it exists alongside natural moral knowledge.[38]

A thoroughly Protestant account of natural law is consistent with the principle of *sola scriptura*, affirming that there is no final authority other than the Bible. In this way, while Protestants can learn much from Roman Catholic writings about natural law, a Protestant account will differ in important respects from the Roman Catholic view of natural law.

Natural Law Is Not Persuasive to Unbelievers

Natural law arguments rarely seem to be persuasive to unbelievers or in public reasoning, so what is the point of employing them? It seems that only those who accept the authority of Scripture accept the teaching of natural law. As Francesca

36. Barrett, *God's Word Alone*, 332–33.
37. Barrett, *God's Word Alone*, 343–44.
38. Johnson, "Biblical Warrant," 197.

Aran Murphy wrote in 2014, "The rational arguments we offer fall on deaf ears. We may as well be citing Scripture."[39] How should the proponent of natural law respond to this objection?

The doctrine of natural law is not primarily about offering persuasive arguments to nonbelievers but about recognizing the existence of a divinely given moral order. It is necessary to distinguish the objective reality of the natural law from its likelihood of being accepted. It is not surprising that many people reject the natural law and do not find it persuasive. Scripture itself teaches that "the mind that is set on the flesh is hostile to God, for it does not submit to God's law; indeed, it cannot. Those who are in the flesh cannot please God" (Rom. 8:7–8). Thus, "not all sins against natural law can be demonstrated to be so by evidence, at least to the satisfaction of all men."[40]

Andrew Walker argues that natural law is more about discipleship than apologetics, helping to articulate the reasons why Christians believe what we believe about morality and how those beliefs are grounded in objective reality.[41] Thus, a doctrine of natural law has value, even if it is rejected outside the community of faith.

Natural Law Attempts to Construct an Autonomous System of Morality

Another objection leveled at the doctrine of natural law by Protestant writers is that it attempts to construct an autonomous or atheological system of morality. According to Jacques

39. Francesca Aran Murphy, "The Church and Civil Marriage," *First Things*, April 2014, https://www.firstthings.com/article/2014/04/the-church-and-civil-marriage.

40. De Vitoria, "On the American Indians," 274.

41. Walker, *Faithful Reason*, 36–37, 41–42.

Ellul, natural law is the idea that nature functions by itself, as though "God originally created the universe with its laws and subsequently abandoned it to its own destiny."[42] Cornelius Van Til argued that if humans are able to accurately know truth solely by means of natural revelation, then there is little need for Scripture.[43] He thought the Roman Catholic approach to reason and natural law, as exemplified especially by Aquinas, was based on a view of human reason as autonomous: "For Van Til, natural law theory is based upon the notion of autonomy—that man is ultimately autonomous and not in need of God."[44]

R. J. Rushdoony argues forcefully that there is no normative law deriving from nature, but only God's law deriving from biblical revelation. For Rushdoony, natural law "rests itself on the ultimacy of man's mind and it appeals to a common rationality in all men." He sees natural law philosophy as holding that natural man "without saving faith, can work his way up to God and a universal law."[45] Some early modern conceptions of natural law probably *did* portray it as belonging to an autonomous moral order.[46] A common narrative is that, commencing with Hugo Grotius, early modern thinkers sought to infer a system of natural law that was not derived from or embedded in a system of divine or eternal law.[47] It is

42. Jacques Ellul, *The Theological Foundations of Law*, trans. Marguerite Wieser (Seabury Press, 1969), 64.

43. Van Til, *Christian Apologetics*, 52. A similar argument is made by Henry Stob, "Natural Law Ethics: An Appraisal," *Calvin Theological Journal* 20, no. 1 (1985): 58.

44. Haines and Fulford, *Natural Law*, 10; Van Til, *The Defense of the Faith*, 132–39.

45. Rousas John Rushdoony, *The Institutes of Biblical Law* (Presbyterian & Reformed, 1973), 685.

46. Grobien, "What Is the Natural Law?," 19; Porter, *Nature as Reason*, 27–29.

47. Haakonssen, "Early Modern Natural Law Theories."

widely held that these conceptions of natural law affirmed the "autonomy of human reason" and that natural law is an "authority-free zone."[48]

However, Van Til's and Rushdoony's criticisms seem to me to be obviously incorrect readings of Aquinas. A more accurate interpretation is that Aquinas believes that divinely implanted human reason is able to perceive the truths that are self-evident from creation. No doubt Aquinas is more optimistic about the powers of human reason than the magisterial Reformers.[49] However, he does not believe that human reason operates autonomously. Scholastic theologians such as Aquinas did not develop natural law principles from purely rational starting points but believed that Scripture "completes and corrects the deliverances of reason."[50] For Aquinas, God is the measure of all things, not humans.[51] Aquinas writes that the whole universe is governed by God's eternal law and argues that natural law is the participation by humans in that law. Human inclinations are the imprint of the eternal law, directing humans to their proper ends (*ST* I-II, 91.1–2).

In any event, it is not the case that natural law constructs an autonomous and self-sufficient system of morality. Natural law is the law of God, not a sphere of autonomous norms: God is the "one universal source of nature and of all things in nature."[52] There is no neutral territory. The moral order is something discerned imperfectly by human reason, through reflection, observation, and education, with our understanding informed by the

48. Rommen, *The Natural Law*, ch. 4; Hittinger, *First Grace*, xii.

49. See, e.g., Matthew J. Tuininga, *Calvin's Political Theology and the Public Engagement of the Church: Christ's Two Kingdoms* (Cambridge University Press, 2017), 104.

50. Porter, *Nature as Reason*, 17, 27.

51. Nielsen, "Examination of the Thomistic Theory," 44, 53.

52. Junius, *Mosaic Polity*, 65; Hemmingsen, *On the Law of Nature*, 27.

Christian tradition and subject to the fundamental authority of Scripture, which alone can provide an accurate and complete knowledge of the moral law. To the extent that humans accurately perceive the nature of that order, it is God's law that we are discerning.[53]

Natural Law Is a Roman Catholic Doctrine

One of the biggest obstacles to accepting natural law for Protestants is that many see natural law as a Roman Catholic doctrine, not consistent with Protestant views of Scripture or soteriology. R. J. Rushdoony considers that the doctrine of natural law is "heretical nonsense."[54] As noted above, there are certainly problems with the doctrine of natural law as articulated by the Roman Catholic Church. However, a genuinely Protestant account of natural law will avoid these errors. Accepting the principle of natural law does not entail acceptance of the pronouncements of the Roman Catholic Church as infallible.

Natural law is not solely a Roman Catholic doctrine: Recent scholarship has begun to recognize that natural law was widely accepted by Protestants until well into the twentieth century, and they did not see it as inconsistent with Protestant teaching.[55] Richard Muller argues:

> The Reformation, in spite of its substantial contribution to the history of doctrine and the shock it delivered to theology and the church in the sixteenth century, was not an attack upon

53. See, e.g., Hooker, *Laws*, 1:167 [3.9.2].

54. Rushdoony, *The Institutes of Biblical Law*, 9; Ellul, *The Theological Foundations of Law*, 12–13.

55. Grabill, *Rediscovering the Natural Law*, ch. 1.

> the whole of medieval theology or upon Christian tradition. The Reformation assaulted a limited spectrum of doctrinal and practical abuses with the intention of reaffirming the values of the historical church catholic. Thus, the mainstream Reformers reconstructed the doctrines of justification and the sacraments and then modified their ideas of the *ordo salutis* and of the church accordingly; but they did not alter the doctrines of God, creation, providence, and Christ, and they maintained the Augustinian tradition concerning predestination, human nature and sin. The reform of individual doctrines, like justification and the sacraments, occurred within the bounds of a traditional, orthodox, and catholic system which, on the grand scale, remained substantively unaltered.[56]

While the Reformation made many changes to Christian doctrine, many doctrines were left largely intact—including natural law. John T. McNeill argues that "there is no real discontinuity between the teaching of the Reformers and that of their predecessors with respect to natural law. Not one of the leaders of the Reformation assails the principle."[57] The Reformers "assumed the natural law as a moral-theological bedrock in their system and maintained continuity with their Catholic counterparts. It is accurate to insist that the Reformation controversies with the Catholic Church were foremost theological and not ethical."[58]

Many writers within the Protestant tradition have accepted the doctrine of natural law, and many have been strongly influenced by Aquinas. An example is George Gillespie, whom I

56. Muller, *Post-Reformation Reformed Dogmatics*, 1:97.

57. John T. McNeill, "Natural Law in the Teaching of the Reformers," *Journal of Religion* 26 (1946): 168.

58. J. Daryl Charles, *Retrieving the Natural Law: A Return to Moral First Things* (Eerdmans, 2008), 114.

have quoted throughout this book. He was a highly regarded Scottish divine who participated in the Westminster Assembly as a commissioner and was a leading advocate of Presbyterian church government. Gillespie's account of the natural law is as follows:

> There are three sorts of things which the law of nature requires of man, as both schoolmen and modern doctors have rightly taught. . . . First . . . the law of nature requires him to seek the conservation of his own being, and to shun or repel such things as may destroy the same. . . . This is, therefore, the first precept of the law of nature, that man seek his own conservation, and avoid his own destruction. Whereupon this conclusion necessarily follows, that he may repel violence with violence. Secondly, as man is a living creature, the law of nature teaches him to propagate and conserve his kind. Whereupon these conclusions do follow, *viz.*, the commixtion [*union*] of male and female, the procreation of children, the educating of them, and providing for them. This nature has taught to man, as a thing common to him with other living creatures.
>
> Thirdly, as man is a creature endued with reason, . . . the law of nature teaches man, to know that there is a God, and that this God is to be worshiped; whereupon it follows, that man should seek to know God, and the manner of His worship. . . . The law of nature teaches man to hold fast friendship and amity with his neighbours, for as much as he is *animal sociale* [social animal]. . . . For the law of nature bids us do to others as we would have others do unto us (Luke 6:31). And from these precepts it follows, that we should not offend other men; that we should keep promises; stand to bargains; give to every man his own, etc. . . . As touching a man's self, the law of nature teaches him that he should not live as a reasonless creature, but that all his actions should be such as may be congruous

> and beseeming for a creature endued with reason. Whereupon it follows, that he should live honestly and virtuously, that he should observe order and decency in all his actions, etc.[59]

Gillespie's debt to Aquinas is clear, following the division of the natural law into three categories. This is an instructive example, because Gillespie's Reformed and Presbyterian credentials are not in doubt—this passage occurs in his *Dispute Against the English-Popish Ceremonies*—and yet he considers an essentially Thomist account of natural law to be consistent with those commitments.

In an article published in 2022, I argued that the *Westminster Confession of Faith* teaches a doctrine of natural law.[60] Although John Calvin is widely recognized to have been pessimistic about the capacities of fallen humankind, he nevertheless thought that some knowledge of the natural law remains: "If the Gentiles by nature have law righteousness engraved upon their minds, we surely cannot say they are utterly blind as to the conduct of life. There is nothing more common than for a man to be sufficiently instructed in a right standard of conduct by natural law."[61] Similarly, he says, "It is a fact that the law of God which we call the moral law is nothing else than a testimony of natural law and of that conscience which God has engraved upon the minds of men."[62]

Reformed theologian Franciscus Junius defines *natural law* in strongly Thomist terms: "The natural law is that which is innate to creatures endowed with reason and informs them with common notions of nature, that is, with principles and conclusions

59. Gillespie, *English-Popish Ceremonies*, 361–62.

60. Benjamin B. Saunders, "Hidden in Plain Sight: Natural Law and the Westminster Confession of Faith," *Westminster Theological Journal* 84 (2022): 177.

61. Calvin, *Institutes of the Christian Religion*, 2.2.22.

62. Calvin, *Institutes of the Christian Religion*, 4.20.16.

adumbrating the eternal law by a certain participation."[63] For Junius, the natural law underlay the Mosaic law, which was a perfect example of the implementation of natural law in its context.

Lutheran theologian Niels Hemmingsen defines *natural law* as follows: "The law of nature is a certain knowledge, imprinted on the minds of men by God, of the principles of knowing and acting, and of the conclusions proved from these principles that are in agreement with the proper end of man. Reason constructs these conclusions from the principles by necessary consequence for the government of human life, so that man may recognize, want, choose, and do the things that are right, and avoid their opposites; and God has bestowed on men the conscience as the witness and judge of all these things."[64]

As a final example, Reformed theologian Girolamo Zanchi defines the natural law as follows:

> Natural law is the will of God, and, consequently, the divine rule and principle for knowing what to do and what not to do. It is, namely, the knowledge of what is good or bad, fair or unfair, upright or shameful, that was inscribed upon the hearts of all people by God himself also after the Fall. For this reason, we are all universally taught what activities should be pursued and what should be avoided; that is, to do one thing and to avoid another, and we know that we are obligated and pushed to act for the glory of God, our own good, and the welfare of our neighbor both in private and in public.[65]

In sum, many Protestant writers have endorsed a doctrine of natural law, seeing no conflict with Protestant views of Scripture and soteriology.

63. Junius, *Mosaic Polity*, 44.
64. Hemmingsen, *On the Law of Nature*, 30.
65. Zanchi, *On the Law in General*, 13–14.

Natural Law Is Not a Distinctively Evangelical Idea

Another prominent strand of Protestant critique of natural law is that it is not a distinctively evangelical idea. Oliver O'Donovan argues that evangelical ethics must be based on the foundation of the gospel of Jesus Christ.[66] Natural law, however, grounds morality in a universal moral order. The New Testament calls Christians to radical, sacrificial, costly discipleship and forgiveness (e.g., Matt. 10:37–39), which appears to go well beyond a universally accessible and reasonable moral law. Natural law may seem to blunt the radical demands of New Testament teaching.

For some, natural law represents the abandonment of a truly evangelical basis for law and justice. Perhaps the most strident critique of natural law came from Karl Barth, whose polemics largely paved the way for the eclipse of natural law in the twentieth century.[67] Barth considers that natural law creates an "autonomous locus of theological and moral reflection that is severed from grace and God's revelation in Jesus Christ," replacing the Christocentric faith of Christianity with a secularized humanism.[68] For Barth, humans have no inherent capacity to know God apart from God's gracious decision to reveal himself to us through the word of God in Christ.[69]

Some argue that Christian ethical and political thinking should be shaped by the cross and resurrection of Christ, and not a minimalist appeal to creation norms accessible by natural reason, which merely reminds the world of what it already knows.[70] Stanley Hauerwas argues that natural law is culturally

66. O'Donovan, *Resurrection and Moral Order*, 11.

67. Grabill, *Rediscovering the Natural Law*, 29–38.

68. Charles, "Protestant Bias Against the Natural Law," 31–32.

69. Stephen J. Wellum, "Karl Barth, Natural Revelation, and Its Implications for Ethics," *Eikon* 2, no. 2 (2020): 129.

70. James K. A. Smith, *Awaiting the King: Reforming Public Theology* (Baker Academic, 2017), 151, 153.

assimilationist and simply underwrites the existing social and political order.[71] Jacques Ellul rejects the idea of a universal moral law that presupposes the ability of non-Christians to accept the will of God; a knowledge of the good is not possible outside of a personal relationship with Christ, revealed through Scripture.[72] Carl F. H. Henry criticizes natural law on the basis that it excludes reference to revelation in determining the content of the moral law. For evangelical Christianity, by contrast, the content of morality is derived from divine revelation and the Bible.[73]

The most obvious response to these critiques is that Scripture itself teaches a concept of natural law. The natural law in Scripture is not precisely the same as the doctrine held by Aquinas or other writers. Nevertheless, Scripture clearly teaches the principle of an objectively meaningful and ordered reality, and that all people are able to imperfectly perceive some aspects of that order.

It is true that in the New Testament a higher standard of conduct is expected of believers than the law of nature.[74] As put by David VanDrunen, Christians are called to live in ways "that go beyond and even confound the natural law."[75] It remains the case, however, that all people are governed by universal moral norms: It would be wrong, needless to say, for Christians to worship false gods, or commit murder or adultery. Paul treats the moral law as binding on believers (Rom. 13:8–10).

71. Stanley Hauerwas, *The Peaceable Kingdom: A Primer in Christian Ethics* (University of Notre Dame Press, 1983), 52–59. See also Adams, "Law of Nature," 88, 94.

72. Ellul, *The Theological Foundations of Law*, 13, 45; Jacques Ellul, *To Will and To Do: An Introduction to Christian Ethics*, trans. Jacob Marques Rollison (James Clarke, 2023), 1:30.

73. Henry, "Natural Law and a Nihilistic Culture," 54, 56.

74. Grotius, *The Rights of War and Peace*, 1:126.

75. VanDrunen, *Natural Law*, 80.

Christians are subject to both the moral (natural) law and the radical demands of New Testament teaching.

It also seems to me that the critiques of Hauerwas and others understate the extent to which natural law is at odds with the prevailing moral practices of any culture and underestimate just how difficult it is to comply with natural law in a fallen world. In every culture there will be beliefs and practices that are consistent in some respects with the natural law. But there will also be practices that are repugnant to the moral law. Natural law does not simply validate the existing social order but critiques it, sometimes radically.

Take, for instance, the paradigmatic natural law institution: marriage. The divorce rate in modern Western countries is nearly 50 percent. For two sinful people to maintain a successful, lifelong marriage requires (among other things) that each spouse puts the interests of the other first and that each be prepared to regularly forgive when offended. This is not wholly different from "kingdom ethics" (see Phil. 2:3–5). Similar comments could be made about obedience to civil government (Rom. 13:1–7; 1 Pet. 2:13–25; Titus 3:1), submission to earthly masters (Col. 3:22–25; Eph. 6:5–8), and obeying parents (Col. 3:20; Eph. 6:1–3).

Is natural law truly evangelical? As noted, O'Donovan argues that evangelical ethics must be based on the gospel. Central to that gospel is the resurrection, which is a vindication and restoration of the created order; the resurrection therefore directs us "back to the creation which it vindicates."[76] That is, for O'Donovan the resurrection is the vindication of the created order, which is central to the idea of natural law. There is thus no choice to be made between "kingdom

76. O'Donovan, *Resurrection and Moral Order*, 11, 31.

ethics" and "creation ethics": "The ethics of the kingdom is the ethics of creation."[77]

Conclusion

The aim of this chapter has been to note some of the main objections leveled at the doctrine of natural law from both within and outside the Christian tradition. I hope to have demonstrated that natural law is a catholic doctrine of the universal church and thoroughly consistent with Protestant teaching.

77. Smith, *Awaiting the King*, 154; Haas, "Creational Ethics Is Public Ethics," 21.

[illegible] and force [illegible]? The ethics of the kingdom or the ethic of creation?

Conclusion

[illegible] the discussion [illegible]

Conclusion

The Relevance of Natural Law Today

This book has attempted to outline a thoroughly Protestant and biblical account of natural law. In this chapter, I argue that natural law can play a valuable role for Christians today.

Objective Moral Order

First, the natural law provides the basis for an objective moral order and the objectivity of moral values. As argued in chapter 8, many people today profess to believe that morality is subjective or relative, but in fact believe in many moral absolutes. For any stable society to exist, it is not possible to do without moral absolutes. This raises some obvious questions: What is the content of these standards? And who decides? If there is no objective moral order to which human law must conform, then we are at the mercy and the will of the lawmaker. Natural law provides a rational and objective basis for morality and law and an objective standard against which to evaluate human civil laws.

In response to the objection that the Bible can provide this objective standard, I have argued that if morality is solely what the Bible declares to be right and wrong, and nothing else, then this leads to two problems. First, morality existed prior to the revealing of the moral law in Scripture; second, those who have never heard the teaching of Scripture are nevertheless accountable for breaching the moral law. The Bible itself recognizes that all people are subject to the moral law and can perceive some aspects of moral truth, although imperfectly, outside Scripture.

Reconciling Law and Order

Law and wisdom are sometimes seen as opposed to each other. Oliver Barclay observes that for many people "Christian ethics seem to be an arbitrary set of rules imposed by a remote God for no very good reason . . . a set of norms imposed on the Christian by virtue of his obedience to Christ, and for no other reason than that God says so."[1] This points to another very important role that natural law can play—namely, explaining the logic, purpose, and rationale of the moral law.

Underlying every ethical command is a rationale, which relates to the moral order, the character of God, and the structure of creation. Natural law "seeks to explain the reasons behind the command so as to give intelligible explanation for morality's reasonableness and obligation. Natural law ethics is thus fundamentally about articulating the underlying and theoretical reasonableness of biblical ethics," thus playing an important role in Christian discipleship.[2]

Three Uses of the Law

The Protestant tradition has traditionally held that the moral law has three uses. Natural law is relevant in each of these three ways.

1. Barclay, "The Nature of Christian Morality," 125.
2. Walker, *Faithful Reason*, 75.

First, the moral law has a theological use in condemning sin, and uncovering and exposing sin, which is the problem that the gospel addresses. The Bible teaches that all people are accountable to God for breaching the moral law, and that we are "without excuse" for doing so (Rom. 1:20; 3:19–20). This can only be possible if the requirements of the law are applicable to all people and have been revealed to all people. Natural law serves to condemn. It explains how all people can be held accountable to the moral law.

Natural law is thus necessary for the gospel, playing an important role, through the conscience, in uncovering and exposing sin. Natural law does not undermine the message of salvation through the gospel, but provides the necessary scaffold.[3] Outside of Christ, all people are dead in their transgressions and sins (Eph. 2:1), do not submit to God's law, and cannot please God (Rom. 8:7–8). God has revealed a righteousness that is apart from the law (Rom. 3:21) so that we are justified by faith alone in Christ (Rom. 3:24, 28; Eph. 2:8–9). A saving knowledge of God is not possible outside Christ, revealed through the Scripture. Natural law, therefore, serves a purpose similar to the theological use of the law in condemning us and awakening us to a knowledge of our sin.

The second is the civil use of the law—namely, that the law restrains people through the coercive mechanisms of civil law and government. Natural law has a vital role to play in the civil realm. While Scripture contains a great deal of teaching about civil government and law, it is not, and is not intended to be, exhaustive. Natural law provides a range of principles that are "a matter of objective reasonableness, not of whim, convention,

3. David VanDrunen, "Natural Law for Reformed Theology: A Proposal for Contemporary Reappropriation," *Journal of Reformed Theology* 9, no. 2 (2015): 129.

or mere 'decision'" and that provide a rational basis for law-making.[4] Civil government and law have enormous potential for good and evil, and so need to be subjected to objective constraints. Natural law serves as a means of holding civil law accountable to an objective standard and counters the view that law is simply the product of the legislative will.

The moral law has a third, didactic use—namely, it guides the believer in the manner of living so as to please God. Natural law can function as a powerful aid to sanctification. God's people are supposed to meditate constantly on the law (e.g., Ps. 1:2). One way of doing that is to reflect on how the law reflects the beauty of God's creation and the moral order, his character, and what is good for humans. We can reflect on how the law promotes the good and enables people to flourish. We can reflect on the harmful and destructive consequences of sin in broken lives and relationships.

Natural law, therefore, can help Christians to see the law not simply as an arbitrary set of commands but as something that conduces to our good and that has a deeper logic and rationale. This can provide a powerful motivation to obey the law.

Interpreting Scripture

The use of symbolic and creational imagery in Scripture suggests that scriptural imagery cannot be understood without carefully reading and meditating on the nature of the created order. The Bible contains many laws, some of which continue to apply today and others that do not. In Leviticus 19, God commanded the Israelites not to steal, deal falsely with, or lie to each other (vv. 11–12). Most Christians would consider

4. Finnis, *Natural Law and Natural Rights*, 290.

that these commands remain binding today. But in the very same chapter God commanded the Israelites not to round off the hair on their temples or mar the edges of their beards and not to tattoo themselves (vv. 27–28). Most Christians would consider that these commands are not binding today. Why is one binding and the other not? Christians have traditionally answered such questions by reference to natural law. Natural law helps us to discern which commands are founded on moral grounds and are applicable to all people and which were specific to Israel.[5] That is, natural law is necessary to interpret Scripture properly.

The Value of Earthly Goods

Christians often seem to have difficulty reasoning and thinking about things that are common features of ordinary life but are not dealt with in much detail in Scripture, including education, sports, exercise, and nutrition. Natural law helps us to properly orient the value of such things and provides a framework for thinking about them.

Natural law theory defines a series of goods that are noninstrumental—that is, they are valuable in their own right and not a means to another end. Such goods include life, health, procreation, knowledge, play, beauty, friendship, sociability, freedom, reason, integrity, authenticity, religion, family, justice, vocation, skillfulness, authenticity, and pleasure.[6] We can, for example, appreciate art because beauty

5. Grobien, "What Is the Natural Law?," 27; James Bannerman, *The Church of Christ: A Treatise on the Nature, Powers, Ordinances, Discipline, and Government of the Christian Church* (Banner of Truth, 1960), 2:406.

6. Finnis, *Natural Law and Natural Rights*, 86–90. See also Walker, *Faithful Reason*, 163–65, listing life (including health), family, friendship, knowledge, aesthetic appreciation (beauty), practical reasonableness, integrity, religion, and

and aesthetic experience are valuable ends in themselves, and it is not necessary to justify this by reference to something else.

Technological Conception of Human Nature

Natural law has a very important role to play today in its understanding of human nature. Technology has reshaped our view of humanity, such that it is now considered that there is no inherent or received meaning in human nature or the body.

A doctrine of natural law, with its emphasis on moral order and the goodness of the physical body, can help counter the technological conception of human nature as malleable and plastic, and respond to the challenges of today's beliefs regarding gender and sexuality.[7]

Natural Law and Church Government

The significant role for natural law in church government is recognized by the *Westminster Confession*, which states that there are some circumstances concerning church government "which are to be ordered by the light of nature" (1.6). Scripture sets out a distinct form of church government (*WCF* 30.1) but is not exhaustive, and so there are many matters relating to church life that need to be determined by human decision.

But many of the determinations that regulate and order the detailed specifics of church life are largely arbitrary—for example, what time should be set for corporate worship or what should be the quorum for a board of management meeting.

play; Crowe, *Natural Law and the Nature of Law*, 35 ("life, health, pleasure, friendship, play, appreciation, understanding, meaning and reasonableness").

7. Trueman, *Rise and Triumph*, 405.

Without a doctrine of natural law, there is little or nothing between the high-level principles of church government set out in Scripture and the largely arbitrary determinations of church codes. Decisions made solely by reference to arbitrary human church codes can be (and frequently are) unjust. Natural law establishes an overriding standard of justice, including principles such as procedural fairness, majority decision-making, and the right of appeal,[8] which can ensure that decisions are made fairly and that unjust decisions can be appealed.[9]

Wisdom

A Protestant account of natural law does not seek to impose a range of extrabiblical directives on oppressed consciences. Rather, natural law recognizes the complexity and richness of the created order and the need for wisdom. It provides a way of moving the conversation beyond a simplistic "Does Scripture prohibit this practice?" especially where Scripture does not directly address a particular topic. Natural law functions as an invitation to wisdom and reflection on the moral order.

For example, there is a practice among barristers in Australia, including Christian barristers, of charging an entire day's fees to attend a court hearing, even if the hearing only lasts part of the day. I acknowledge that there are situations where this practice may be justified (for example, where a barrister needs to block out an entire day and so is unable to carry out

8. Coldwell, *Jus Divinum Regiminis Ecclesiastici*, 62.

9. See further Benjamin B. Saunders, "Why Church Government Needs a Doctrine of Natural Law," in *Jurisprudence and Theology: The Australian School*, ed. Jonathan Crowe, Constance Youngwon Lee, and Joshua Neoh (Routledge, 2026).

other work), but it can mean that barristers charge a full day's rate (amounting to thousands of dollars) for a couple of hours of work, when they could (and probably do) return to chambers and carry out work for other clients, for which they also charge handsomely.

This practice is possible because the standard costs agreement between barristers and clients enables lawyers to do it. I asked a friend (who is a Christian, and a barrister, and who does not generally adopt this practice) about the morality of this. His response was that it is simply a matter of the contractual arrangement between barrister and client: If the costs agreement allows a barrister to charge for the full day for a part day's work, then they are entitled to do so.

What might a natural law approach say? First, there is an overarching standard of justice that applies to commercial dealings. Even if a particular practice is permitted or common in a particular commercial context, that does not mean that it is right. Second, natural law writers have said that a "man who keeps more for himself than he needs is guilty of theft."[10] While hyperbolic, this clearly speaks to the amassing of wealth at others' expense. Third, the law of nature bids us do to others as we would have others do to us. Being charged for work not actually carried out is obviously in breach of this. Unless there is good reason, this practice is clearly immoral.

Could we have reached this conclusion by aid of Scripture alone? Yes, probably. But apparently not, given the number of Christian barristers who seem happy to adhere to this practice. Because there is no Bible verse directly prohibiting this practice, many Christians feel free to adopt it.

10. Tierney, *The Idea of Natural Rights*, 70.

Natural Law and the Knowledge of God

Finally, natural law points us to the reality of the created order as reflecting the glory of the God who made that order, and made it "very good." The world is not formless matter but bears the imprint of the divine character. Puritan theologian Richard Baxter writes that God has "made an Impress of his minde upon the Creation" and given humans a capacity to perceive what is revealed in that creation.[11] Natural law invites us to read the book of nature and the book of Scripture as manifestations of God's wisdom and character.

It also invites us to reflect on the beauty of the created order in light of Scripture and to read Scripture as harmonious with that order. Elaine Scarry writes that beauty "fills the mind yet invites the search for something beyond itself, something larger or something of the same scale with which it needs to be brought in relation." Beautiful things "carry greetings from other worlds within them."[12] Scripture and natural law direct us to read creation through new eyes, viewing the nature of reality as a symbolic representation of God: "The doctrine of creation means that every created item, and also the created order as a whole, reflects the character of the God who created it. In other words, everything in the creation, and the creation as a whole, points to God. Everything is a sign or symbol of God."[13]

Natural law should give Christians greater confidence in Scripture, which is not a series of arbitrary commands but reflects the objective order of reality, and should drive us to worship and adore its Creator.

11. Richard Baxter, *A Holy Commonwealth* (Thomas Underhill and Francis Tyton, 1659), 50.

12. Elaine Scarry, *On Beauty and Being Just* (Princeton University Press, 1999), 29, 31, 47, 52.

13. Jordan, *Through New Eyes*, 30.

Theses[1]

Thesis 1: God is the source of all law and justice, and all good laws flow from God.

Thesis 2: Natural law is the moral order according to which God has created all things. That order defines the proper ends of human nature, the good that is to be pursued, and the evil to be avoided.

Thesis 3: One aspect of the created moral order is the rules or precepts that are known as the moral law (such as "you shall have no other gods before me" and "you shall not murder"). These precepts express important aspects of the moral order, but the moral order is broader than the precepts of the moral law.

Thesis 4: The natural law was given or implanted at creation and existed prior to the revelation of the moral law recorded in Scripture.

Thesis 5: Scripture contains a renewed and authoritative statement of the natural law.

Thesis 6: The Decalogue is a perfect summary of the content of the moral law (and the natural law). However, the Decalogue and the natural law are not identical.

1. This list draws from the theses set out in Zanchi, *On the Law in General*.

Thesis 7: The principles of the natural law are preceptive, self-evident, indemonstrable, noninstrumental, and foundational principles of morality and practical reason.

Thesis 8: The work of the moral law is written on every human heart, and the conscience bears witness to it. Humans suppress the knowledge of the natural law in unrighteousness; however, that knowledge cannot be completely erased.

Thesis 9: It follows from thesis 8 that any person's knowledge of the moral law by means of the light of nature alone is always incomplete and defective. Scripture is necessary to attain an accurate and complete knowledge of the moral law.

Thesis 10: Human ability to act consistently with the precepts of the natural law is corrupted by sin.

Thesis 11: It follows from theses 9 and 10 that it is not possible for humans to attain salvation solely through natural law. In order to attain a knowledge of those things requisite for salvation, both the revelation of Scripture and heart-change wrought by the Holy Spirit are necessary.

Thesis 12: Scripture is the only inspired, supreme, sufficient, and final authority in matters of faith and life. Scripture alone contains the infallible revelation of the moral law.

Thesis 13: There is no person or body of persons that has the power to authoritatively interpret and declare the content of the natural law and whose teachings are necessary for salvation.

Thesis 14: There are some moral norms that are not specifically taught in Scripture but that are necessary to affirm as part of the natural law. Care is needed when affirming the existence of such norms; the articulation of such norms must be recognized to be subordinate to the authority of the Bible.

Thesis 15: Examples of extrabiblical precepts include that slavery, discrimination on ethnic or racial grounds, suicide, euthanasia, cannibalism, torture, and polygamy are morally wrong; prisoners of war should be treated humanely; a person may use proportionate force in self-defense; consent is necessary in order for a valid contract to come into existence; no person ought to judge a matter in which they have a personal interest.

Thesis 16: Natural law is the law of God. The doctrine of natural law does not teach that human reason is autonomous, and it does not attempt to construct an autonomous system of morality.

Thesis 17: Civil laws are necessary to restrain sin, and also because the natural law is indeterminate. Civil laws apply the principles of the moral law in particular contexts and attach legally enforceable consequences.

Thesis 18: Laws enacted by civil governments ought to be consistent with the natural law. Human laws that conflict with natural law are defective and may be invalid. Civil laws that give effect to the natural law are morally binding.

Acknowledgments

Thanks to Simon Kennedy for encouragement and helpful conversations, and to J. Budziszewski for answering various questions about natural law. I am grateful to David VanDrunen and Matthew Levering for reading and providing valuable comments on earlier versions of this book and to Elliot Ritzema for his detailed engagement with the manuscript.

I also express my thanks to Deakin University Library for providing many sources used in researching this book and to the Reformed Theological College in Geelong for access to resources.

Any opinions expressed in this book are the author's alone.

S. D. G.

Recommended Reading

Aquinas, Thomas. *Summa Theologica*. I-II, questions 90–108.

Budziszewski, J. *What We Can't Not Know: A Guide*. Ignatius Press, 2010.

Covington, Jesse, Bryan T. McGraw, and Micah Watson. *Hopeful Realism: Evangelical Natural Law and Democratic Politics*. IVP Academic, 2025.

de Vitoria, Francisco. *Political Writings*. Edited by Anthony Pagden. Cambridge University Press, 1991.

Grabill, Stephen J. *Rediscovering the Natural Law in Reformed Theological Ethics*. Eerdmans, 2006.

Hemmingsen, Niels. *On the Law of Nature: A Demonstrative Method*. CLP Academic, 2018.

Junius, Franciscus. *The Mosaic Polity*. Edited by Andrew M. McGinnis. Translated by Todd M. Rester. CLP Academic, 2015.

McCall, Brian M. *The Architecture of Law: Rebuilding Law in the Classical Tradition*. University of Notre Dame Press, 2018.

Porter, Jean. *Natural and Divine Law: Reclaiming the Tradition for Christian Ethics*. Eerdmans, 1999.

Suárez, Francisco. *Selections from Three Works*. Edited by Thomas Pink. Translated by Gwladys L. Williams et al. Liberty Fund, 2015.

VanDrunen, David. *Divine Covenants and Moral Order: A Biblical Theology of Natural Law*. Eerdmans, 2014.

VanDrunen, David. *Natural Law: A Short Companion*. B&H Academic, 2023.

VanDrunen, David. *Politics After Christendom: Political Theology in a Fractured World*. Zondervan, 2020.

Walker, Andrew T. *Faithful Reason: Natural Law Ethics for God's Glory and Our Good*. B&H Academic, 2024.

Walker, Andrew T., and Ryan T. Anderson, eds. *Natural Law: Five Views*. Zondervan Academic, 2025.

Zanchi, Girolamo. *On the Law in General*. Translated by Jeffrey J. Veenstra. CLP Academic, 2012.

Glossary

Civil law: as used in this book, "civil law" means law made by a civil government.

Conscience: the faculty that applies the law of God to human conduct, approving that which is done rightly and condemning transgressions.

Divine law: law commanded or revealed in Scripture.

Eternal law: as defined by Aquinas, the rational pattern of the divine wisdom that directs all things to their proper end.

Law: an ordinance of reason for the common good, made by the one who has care of the community, and promulgated.

Law of nations: in natural law thought, the law common to civilized nations.

Light of nature: the inbuilt witness to the natural law, or reason.

Moral law: the unchanging and universally applicable standard of right and wrong.

Natural law: the moral order according to which God has created all things, which defines the proper ends of human nature, the good that is to be pursued, and the evil to be avoided.

Positive law: law made by a lawful authority (whether civil or ecclesiastical) at a particular time as a determination of the natural law.

Practical reason: reason oriented to action.

Prudence: the virtue that grasps the truths of the moral law and determines appropriate courses of action.

Speculative reason: reason directed to knowing things as they are.

Bibliography

Adams, James Luther. “The Law of Nature: Some General Considerations.” *Journal of Religion* 25, no. 2 (1945): 88–96.

Adolphe, Jane, Robert Fastiggi, and Michael Vacca, eds. *St. Paul, the Natural Law, and Contemporary Legal Theory*. Lexington Books, 2012.

Anderson, Owen. *The Natural Moral Law: The Good After Modernity*. Cambridge University Press, 2012.

Angier, Tom, ed. *The Cambridge Companion to Natural Law Ethics*. Cambridge University Press, 2019.

Aquinas, Thomas. *On Kingship, to the King of Cyprus*. Translated by Gerald B. Phelan. Pontifical Institute of Mediaeval Studies, 1949.

Aquinas, Thomas. *Political Writings*. Edited by R. W. Dyson. Cambridge University Press, 2020.

Aquinas, Thomas. *Summa Contra Gentiles*. Translated by Vernon J. Bourke. University of Notre Dame Press, 1975.

Aquinas, Thomas. *Summa Theologica*. Translated by Fathers of the English Dominican Province. Maria Press, 1981.

Arkes, Hadley. *First Things: An Inquiry Into the First Principles of Morals and Justice*. Princeton University Press, 1986.

Backus, Irena. “Calvin’s Concept of Natural and Roman Law.” *Calvin Theological Journal* 38 (2003): 7.

Baker, Robert C., ed. *Natural Law: A Lutheran Reappraisal*. Concordia Publishing House, 2011.

Ballor, Jordan J. "A Society of Mutual Aid: Natural Law and Subsidiarity in Early Modern Reformed Perspective." In *Law and Religion: The Legal Teachings of the Catholic and Protestant Reformations*. Edited by Wim Decock et al. Vandenhoeck & Ruprecht, 2014.

Banner, Stuart. *The Decline of Natural Law: How American Lawyers Once Used Natural Law and Why They Stopped*. Oxford University Press, 2021.

Barr, James. *Biblical Faith and Natural Theology*. Clarendon Press, 1993.

Barr, James. "Biblical Law and the Question of Natural Theology." In *Bible and Interpretation: The Collected Essays of James Barr*. Oxford University Press, 2014.

Barth, Karl. *Church Dogmatics*. Translated by G. W. Bromiley. T&T Clark, 1961.

Baur, Michael. "Law and Natural Law." In *The Oxford Handbook of Aquinas*, edited by Brian Davies and Eleonore Stump. Oxford University Press, 2014.

Berquist, Richard. *From Human Dignity to Natural Law: An Introduction*. Catholic University of America Press, 2019.

Black, Rufus. *Christian Moral Realism: Natural Law, Narrative, Virtue, and the Gospel*. Oxford University Press, 2000.

Black, Rufus, and Nigel Biggar, eds. *The Revival of Natural Law: Philosophical, Theological and Ethical Responses to the Finnis-Grisez School*. Ashgate, 2001.

Braaten, Carl E. "Protestants and Natural Law." *First Things* 19 (January 1, 1992): 25.

Brunner, Emil. *Justice and Social Order*. Translated by Mary Hottinger. Lutterworth Press, 1945.

Brunner, Emil, and Karl Barth, *Natural Theology*. Translated by Peter Fraenkel. Geoffrey Bles, 1946.

Budziszewski, J. *Commentary on Thomas Aquinas's Treatise on Divine Law*. Cambridge University Press, 2021.

Budziszewski, J. *Commentary on Thomas Aquinas's Treatise on Law*. Cambridge University Press, 2014.

Budziszewski, J. *Natural Law for Lawyers*. Alliance Defending Freedom, 2019.

Budziszewski, J. *The Revenge of Conscience: Politics and the Fall of Man*. Wipf and Stock, 2010.

Budziszewski, J. *What We Can't Not Know: A Guide*. Ignatius Press, 2010.

Budziszewski, J. *Written on the Heart: The Case for Natural Law*. IVP Academic, 1997.

Bullinger, Heinrich. *The Decades of Henry Bullinger*. Edited by Thomas Harding. Reformation Heritage Books, 2004.

Burton, Simon J. G. "Samuel Rutherford's Euthyphro Dilemma: A Reformed Perspective on the Scholastic Natural Law Tradition." In *Reformed Orthodoxy in Scotland: Essays on Scottish Theology, 1560–1775*. T&T Clark, 2015.

Catechism of the Catholic Church. St Pauls Publishing, 1994.

Chappell, Sophie Grace. *Understanding Human Goods*. Edinburgh University Press, 1998.

Charles, J. Daryl. *Retrieving the Natural Law: A Return to Moral First Things*. Eerdmans, 2008.

Charles, J. Daryl. *Natural Law and Religious Freedom: The Role of Moral First Things in Grounding and Protecting the First Freedom*. Routledge, 2018.

Chartier, Gary. *Economic Justice and Natural Law*. Cambridge University Press, 2009.

Clark, R. Scott. "Calvin and the Lex Naturalis." *Stulos Theological Journal* 6 (1998): 1–22.

Cooper, Kody W., and Justin Buckley Dyer. *The Classical and Christian Origins of American Politics: Political Theology, Natural Law, and the American Founding*. Cambridge University Press, 2022.

Corwin, E. S. "The 'Higher Law' Background of American Constitutional Law." *Harvard Law Review* 42, no. 3 (1929): 365.

Covell, Charles. *The Defence of Natural Law*. St. Martin's Press, 1992.

Covington, Jesse, Bryan T. McGraw, and Micah Watson. *Hopeful Realism: Evangelical Natural Law and Democratic Politics*. IVP Academic, 2025.

Covington, Jesse, Bryan T. McGraw, and Micah Watson, eds. *Natural Law and Evangelical Political Thought*. Lexington Books, 2012.

Cromartie, Michael, ed. *A Preserving Grace: Protestants, Catholics, and Natural Law*. Eerdmans, 1997.

Crowe, Jonathan. *Natural Law and the Nature of Law*. Cambridge University Press, 2019.

Crowe, Jonathan, and Constance Youngwon Lee, eds. *Research Handbook on Natural Law Theory*. Edward Elgar, 2019.

Crowe, Michael Bertram. *The Changing Profile of the Natural Law*. Nijhoff, 1977.

Culverwell, Nathaniel. *An Elegant and Learned Discourse of the Light of Nature*. Edited by Robert A. Greene and Hugh MacCallum. Liberty Fund, 2001.

de Vattel, Emer. *The Law of Nations, or, Principles of the Law of Nature, Applied to the Conduct and Affairs of Nations and Sovereigns*. Edited by Béla Kapossy and Richard Whatmore. Liberty Fund, 2008.

de Vitoria, Francisco. *Political Writings*. Edited by Anthony Pagden. Cambridge University Press, 1991.

D'Entreves, A. P. *Natural Law: An Introduction to Legal Philosophy*. 2nd ed. Hutchinson & Co., 1970.

Doe, Norman, ed. *Christianity and Natural Law: An Introduction*. Cambridge University Press, 2017.

Duke, George, and Robert P. George, eds. *The Cambridge Companion to Natural Law Jurisprudence*. Cambridge University Press, 2017.

Ellul, Jacques. *The Theological Foundations of Law*. Translated by Marguerite Wieser. Seabury Press, 1969.

Emon, Anver M. *Natural Law: A Jewish, Christian, and Islamic Trialogue*. Oxford University Press, 2014.

Finnis, John. *Aquinas: Moral, Legal, and Political Theory*. Oxford University Press, 1998.

Finnis, John. "Law, Morality and 'Sexual Orientation.'" *Notre Dame Law Review* 69 (1994): 1049.

Finnis, John. "The Good of Marriage and the Morality of Sexual Relations: Some Philosophical and Historical Observations." *American Journal of Jurisprudence* 42 (1998): 97.

Finnis, John. *Natural Law and Natural Rights*. 2nd ed. Oxford University Press, 2011.

Finnis, John. "The Rights and Wrongs of Abortion: A Reply to Judith Thomson." *Philosophy and Public Affairs* 2 (1973): 117.

Finnis, John, Germain Grisez, and Joseph Boyle. "Practical Principles, Moral Truth, and Ultimate Ends." *American Journal of Jurisprudence* 32, no. 1 (1987): 128.

Forsyth, Andrew. *Common Law and Natural Law in America: From the Puritans to the Legal Realists.* Cambridge University Press, 2019.

Fortescue, John. *On the Laws and Governance of England.* Edited by Shelley Lockwood. Cambridge University Press, 1997.

George, Robert P. *In Defense of Natural Law.* Oxford University Press, 1999.

George, Robert P. *Making Men Moral: Civil Liberties and Public Morality.* Oxford University Press, 1993.

George, Robert P. "Natural Law." *American Journal of Jurisprudence* 52 (2007): 55.

George, Robert P. "Natural Law." *Harvard Journal of Law & Public Policy* 31, no. 1 (2008): 172.

George, Robert P. "Natural Law Ethics." In *Companion to Philosophy of Religion*, edited by Philip L. Quinn and Charles Taliaferro. Wiley-Blackwell, 1999.

George, Robert P., ed. *Natural Law Theory: Contemporary Essays.* Clarendon Press, 1992.

Gibbs, Lee W. "The Puritan Natural Law Theory of William Ames." *Harvard Theological Review* 64 (1971): 37.

Gillespie, George. *A Dispute Against the English-Popish Ceremonies Obtruded on the Church of Scotland.* Edited by Chris Coldwell. Naphtali Press, 2013.

Gómez-Lobo, Alfonso. *Morality and the Human Goods.* Georgetown University Press, 2002.

Grabill, Stephen J. "Natural Law and the Noetic Effects of Sin: The Faculty of Reason in Francis Turretin's Theological Anthropology." *Westminster Theological Journal* 67, no. 2 (2005): 261.

Grabill, Stephen J. *Rediscovering the Natural Law in Reformed Theological Ethics.* Eerdmans, 2006.

Gratian, *The Treatise on Laws with the Ordinary Gloss.* Translated by Augustine Thompson and James Gordley. Catholic University of America Press, 1993.

Greene, Robert A. "Synderesis, the Spark of Conscience, in the English Renaissance." *Journal of the History of Ideas* 52, no. 2 (1991): 195–219.

Grisez, Germain. "The First Principle of Practical Reason: A Commentary on the *Summa Theologiae*, 1–2, Question 94, Article 2." *Natural Law Forum* 10 (1965): 175.

Grisez, Germain. *The Way of the Lord Jesus: Christian Moral Principles*. 3 vols. Franciscan Press, 1997.

Grisez, Germain, Joseph Boyle, John Finnis, and William May, "Every Marital Act Ought to Be Open to New Life: Toward a Clearer Understanding." *The Thomist* 52 (1988): 365.

Grotius, Hugo. *The Rights of War and Peace*. Edited by Richard Tuck. 3 vols. Liberty Fund, 2005 [1625].

Gustafson, James M. *Protestant and Roman Catholic Ethics: Prospects for Rapprochement*. University of Chicago Press, 1978.

Haakonssen, Knud. *Natural Law and Moral Philosophy: From Grotius to the Scottish Enlightenment*. Cambridge University Press, 1996.

Haines, David, and Andrew A. Fulford. *Natural Law: A Brief Introduction and Biblical Defense*. Davenant Press, 2017.

Hale, Matthew. *Of the Law of Nature*. Edited by David S. Sytsma. CLP Academic, 2015.

Hale, Matthew. *On the Law of Nature, Reason, and Common Law: Selected Jurisprudential Writings*. Edited by Gerald J. Postema. Oxford University Press, 2017.

Hauerwas, Stanley. *The Peaceable Kingdom: A Primer in Christian Ethics*. University of Notre Dame Press, 1983.

Heimbach, Daniel R. "Natural Law in the Public Square." *Liberty University Law Review* 2, no. 3 (2008): 685–702.

Helm, Paul. *Human Nature from Calvin to Edwards*. Reformation Heritage Books, 2018.

Helm, Paul. *John Calvin's Ideas*. Oxford University Press, 2004.

Helmholz, R. H. *Natural Law in Court: A History of Legal Theory in Practice*. Harvard University Press, 2015.

Hemmingsen, Niels. *On the Law of Nature: A Demonstrative Method*. CLP Academic, 2018.

Henry, Carl F. H. *Christian Personal Ethics*. 2nd ed. Eerdmans, 1977.

Henry, Carl F. H. "Natural Law and a Nihilistic Culture." *First Things* (January 1995): 54.

Hittinger, Russell. *The First Grace: Rediscovering the Natural Law in a Post-Christian World*. ISI Books, 2007.

Hochstrasser, T. J. *Natural Law Theories in the Early Enlightenment*. Cambridge University Press, 2000.

Hooker, Richard. *Of the Laws of Ecclesiastical Polity: A Critical Edition with Modern Spelling*. Edited by Arthur Stephen McGrade. Oxford University Press, 2013.

Jackson, Bernard S. "The Jewish View of Natural Law." *Journal of Jewish Studies* 52 (2001): 136–45.

James of Viterbo. *De Regimine Christiano: A Critical Edition and Translation*. Translated by R. W. Dyson. Brill, 2009.

Jensen, Steven J. *Knowing the Natural Law: From Precepts and Inclinations to Deriving Oughts*. Catholic University of America Press, 2015.

John of Paris, *On Royal and Papal Power*. Translated by J. A. Watt. Pontifical Institute of Mediaeval Studies, 1971.

Junius, Franciscus. *The Mosaic Polity*. Edited by Andrew M. McGinnis. Translated by Todd M. Rester. CLP Academic, 2015.

Kennedy, Simon P. *Reforming the Law of Nature: The Secularisation of Political Thought, 1532–1689*. Edinburgh University Press, 2022.

Kirby, W. J. Torrance. "Richard Hooker's Theory of Natural Law in the Context of Reformation Theology." *Sixteenth Century Journal* 30, no. 3 (1999): 681.

Koterski, Joseph. *Natural Law and Human Nature*. Great Courses, 2002.

Lee, Constance Y. "The Spark That Still Shines: John Calvin on Conscience and Natural Law." *Oxford Journal of Law and Religion* 8 (2019): 615–40.

Lee, Patrick. "God and New Natural Law Theory." *National Catholic Bioethics Quarterly* 19, no. 2 (Summer 2019): 280.

Levering, Matthew. *Biblical Natural Law: A Theocentric and Teleological Approach*. Oxford University Press, 2008.

Levering, Matthew, and Marcus Plested, eds. *The Oxford Handbook of the Reception of Aquinas*. Oxford University Press, 2021.

Lewis, C. S. *The Abolition of Man*. 1947. Reprint, HarperOne, 2015.

Lisska, Anthony J. *Aquinas's Theory of Natural Law: An Analytic Reconstruction*. Clarendon Press, 1996.

Littlejohn, Bradford. "Cutting Through the Fog in the Channel: Hooker, Junius, and a Reformed Theology of Law." In *Richard Hooker and Reformed Orthodoxy*, edited by W. Bradford Littlejohn and Scott N. Kindred-Barnes. Vandenhoeck & Ruprecht, 2017.

Luscombe, D. E. "Natural Morality and Natural Law." In *The Cambridge History of Later Medieval Philosophy: From the Rediscovery of Aristotle to the Disintegration of Scholasticism, 1100–1600*, edited by Norman Kretzmann et al. Cambridge University Press, 1982.

Maritain, Jacques. "Lectures on Natural Law." In *The Collected Works of Jacques Maritain*, vol. 6. University of Notre Dame Press, 1986.

Maritain, Jacques. *Man and the State*. University of Chicago Press, 1951.

Maritain, Jacques. *Natural Law: Reflections on Theory and Practice*. St. Augustine's Press, 1952.

Maritain, Jacques. *The Person and the Common Good*. Translated by John J. Fitzgerald. Charles Scribner's Sons, 1947.

Maritain, Jacques. *The Rights of Man and Natural Law*. Translated by Doris C. Anson. Gordian Press, 1971.

McCall, Brian M. *The Architecture of Law: Rebuilding Law in the Classical Tradition*. University of Notre Dame Press, 2018.

McInerny, Ralph. "The Principles of Natural Law." *American Journal of Jurisprudence* 25 (1980): 1.

McNeill, John T. "Natural Law in the Teaching of the Reformers." *Journal of Religion* 26, no. 3 (1946): 168–82.

McNeill, John T. "Natural Law in the Thought of Luther." *Church History* 10 (1941): 211.

Melanchthon, Philip. *The Chief Theological Topics: Loci Praecipui Theologici 1559*. 2nd ed. Translated by J. A. O Preus. Concordia Publishing House, 2011.

Moroney, Stephen K. *The Noetic Effects of Sin: An Historical and Contemporary Exploration of How Sin Affects Our Thinking*. Lexington Books, 2000.

Murphy, Mark C. *Natural Law and Practical Rationality*. Cambridge University Press, 2001.

Murphy, Mark C. *Natural Law in Jurisprudence and Politics*. Cambridge University Press, 2006.

Murphy, Mark C. "Natural Law Jurisprudence." *Legal Theory* 9 (2003): 241–67.

Murphy, Mark C. "Two Unhappy Dilemmas for Natural Law Jurisprudence." *American Journal of Jurisprudence* 60, no. 2 (2015): 1–21.

Murray, John Courtney. *We Hold These Truths: Catholic Reflections on the American Proposition*. Rowman and Littlefield, 1960.

Novak, David. *Natural Law in Judaism*. Cambridge University Press, 1998.

Oakley, Francis. *Natural Law, Conciliarism, and Consent in the Late Middle Ages: Studies in Ecclesiastical and Intellectual History*. Variorum Reprints, 1984.

Oakley, Francis. *Natural Law, Laws of Nature, Natural Rights: Continuity and Discontinuity in the History of Ideas*. Bloomsbury, 2005.

Oderberg, David S. "The Metaphysical Foundations of Natural Law." In *Natural Moral Law in Contemporary Society*. Edited by Holger Zaborowski. Catholic University of America Press, 2010.

O'Donovan, Joan Lockwood. *Theology of Law and Authority in the English Reformation*. Scholars Press, 1991.

O'Donovan, Oliver, and Joan Lockwood O'Donovan, eds. *From Irenaeus to Grotius: A Sourcebook in Christian Political Thought*. Eerdmans, 1999.

Pope, Stephen J. "Natural Law and Christian Ethics." In *The Cambridge Companion to Christian Ethics*, edited by Robin Gill. Cambridge University Press, 2001.

Porter, Jean. "Does the Natural Law Provide a Universally Valid Morality?" In *Intractable Disputes About the Natural Law*, edited by Lawrence S. Cunningham. Notre Dame University Press, 2009.

Porter, Jean. *Natural and Divine Law: Reclaiming the Tradition for Christian Ethics*. Eerdmans, 1999.

Porter, Jean. *Nature as Reason: A Thomistic Theory of the Natural Law*. Eerdmans, 2005.

Ptolemy of Lucca. *On the Government of Rulers: De Regimine Principum*. Translated by James M. Blythe. University of Pennsylvania Press, 1997.

Rice, Charles E. *Fifty Questions on the Natural Law*. Ignatius Press, 1999.

Rommen, Heinrich A. *The Natural Law: A Study in Legal and Social History and Philosophy*. Translated by Thomas R. Hanley. Liberty Fund, 1998.

Ross, Richard J. "Distinguishing Eternal from Transient Law: Natural Law and the Judicial Laws of Moses." *Past & Present* 217 (2012): 79.

Saunders, Benjamin B. "Hidden in Plain Sight: Natural Law and the Westminster Confession of Faith." *Westminster Theological Journal* 84 (2022): 177–202.

Schreiner, Susan E. *The Theater of His Glory: Nature and the Natural Order in the Thought of John Calvin*. Baker, 1995.

Sinnema, Donald. "The Discipline of Ethics in Early Reformed Orthodoxy." *Calvin Theological Journal* 28 (1993): 10.

Stob, Henry. "Natural Law Ethics: An Appraisal." *Calvin Theological Journal* 20, no. 1 (1985): 58.

Stonebraker, Johnathan, and Sarah Irving, "Natural Law and Protestantism: A Historical Reassessment and Its Contemporary Significance." *Oxford Journal of Law and Religion* 4 (2015): 421–41.

Suárez, Francisco. "A Treatise on Laws and God the Lawgiver." In *Selections from Three Works*. Edited by Thomas Pink. Translated by Gwladys L. Williams et al. Liberty Fund, 2015.

Thomasius, Christian. *Institutes of Divine Jurisprudence, with Selections from Foundations of the Law of Nature and Nations*. Edited and translated by Thomas Ahnert. Liberty Fund, 2011.

Tierney, Brian. *The Idea of Natural Rights: Studies on Natural Rights, Natural Law, and Church Law, 1150–1625*. Eerdmans, 1997.

Tuck, Richard. *Natural Rights Theories: Their Origin and Development*. Cambridge University Press, 1979.

VanDrunen, David. *A Biblical Case for Natural Law*. Acton Institute, 2006.

VanDrunen, David. *Divine Covenants and Moral Order: A Biblical Theology of Natural Law*. Eerdmans, 2014.

VanDrunen, David. *Natural Law: A Short Companion*. B&H Academic, 2023.

VanDrunen, David. *Natural Law and the Two Kingdoms: A Study in the Development of Reformed Social Thought*. Eerdmans, 2010.

VanDrunen, David. "Natural Law for Reformed Theology: A Proposal for Contemporary Reappropriation." *Journal of Reformed Theology* 9, no. 2 (2015): 129.

VanDrunen, David. *Politics After Christendom: Political Theology in a Fractured World*. Zondervan, 2020.

VanDrunen, David. "The Use of Natural Law in Early Calvinist Resistance Theory." *Journal of Law and Religion* 21, no. 1 (2006): 143.

von Pufendorf, Samuel. *Two Books of the Elements of Universal Jurisprudence*. Edited by Ian Hunter and Thomas Behme. Translated by William Abbott Oldfather. Liberty Fund, 2009.

von Pufendorf, Samuel. *The Whole Duty of Man According to the Law of Nature*. Edited by Ian Hunter and David Saunders. Translated by Andrew Tooke. Liberty Fund, 2003 [1691].

Vos, Geerhardus. *Natural Theology*. Translated by Albert Gootjes. Reformation Heritage Books, 2022.

Walker, Andrew T. *Faithful Reason: Natural Law Ethics for God's Glory and Our Good*. B&H Academic, 2024.

Walker, Andrew T., ed. *Social Conservatism for the Common Good: A Protestant Engagement with Robert P. George*. Crossway, 2023.

Walker, Andrew T., and Casey Hough. "Toward a Baptist Natural Law Conception of the Common Good." *Southwestern Journal of Theology* 63, no. 1 (Fall 2020): 153–74.

Walker, Andrew T., and Ryan T. Anderson, eds. *Natural Law: Five Views*. Zondervan Academic, 2025.

Wannenwetsch, Bernd. "Creation and Ethics: On the Legitimacy and Limitation of Appeals to 'Nature' in Christian Moral Reasoning." In *Within the Love of God: Essays on the Doctrine of God in Honour of Paul S. Fiddes*, edited by Anthony Clarke and Andrew Moore. Oxford University Press, 2014.

Westerman, Pauline C. *The Disintegration of Natural Law Theory: Aquinas to Finnis*. Brill, 1997.

Wolfe, Christopher, and Steven Brust, eds. *Natural Law Today: The Present State of the Perennial Philosophy*. Lexington Books, 2018.

Yoder, John Howard. *The Politics of Jesus*. Eerdmans, 1972.

Zanchi, Girolamo. *On the Law in General*. Translated by Jeffrey J. Veenstra. CLP Academic, 2012.

Benjamin B. Saunders (PhD, University of Queensland) is an associate professor in law at Deakin Law School, Australia.